Pizza Vending Machine Business

Revolutionizing Fast Food: A Comprehensive Guide to Launching and Managing Pizza Vending Machines

Alex Romano

Copyright © 2024 by Alex Romano

All rights reserved.

No part of this publication may be reproduced, stored in a retrieval system, or transmitted in any form or by any means, electronic, mechanical, photocopying, recording, or otherwise, without the prior written permission of the publisher, except in the case of brief quotations embodied in critical reviews and certain other noncommercial uses permitted by copyright law.

The information contained in this book is for general informational purposes only. While every effort has been made to ensure the accuracy and completeness of the information presented, the author and publisher make no warranties or representations of any kind regarding the accuracy, timeliness, or completeness of the content. Readers are encouraged to consult with professional advisors for specific guidance tailored to their individual circumstances.

First Edition

Author Bio

Alex Romano is an experienced entrepreneur and specialist in the field of automated food services. With over a decade of experience in the vending machine industry, Alex has become a recognized authority on innovative food solutions and automated retail technology. He holds an MBA from Bocconi School of Management and has collaborated with several successful startups focused on revolutionizing food delivery systems.

Alex began his career in the food service industry, where he quickly recognized the potential of automation to enhance efficiency and customer experience. He has been instrumental in launching multiple high-profile vending machine projects, including those integrating cutting-edge technologies to offer customized and fresh food options.

In addition to his practical experience, Alex has contributed to various industry publications and has been a keynote speaker at numerous conferences on automation and food technology. His deep understanding of market trends, combined with his passion for innovation, has made him a sought-after consultant for businesses looking to enter or expand in the vending machine market.

Through his writing and speaking engagements, Alex aims to share his expertise and insights, helping entrepreneurs and business leaders navigate the complexities of the vending industry. His book, Pizza Vending Machine Business, provides a comprehensive guide to launching and managing automated pizza vending machines, offering practical advice, industry trends, and strategies for success.

When he is not consulting or writing, Alex enjoys exploring emerging food technologies and contributing to sustainable food practices. He is dedicated to driving innovation in the food service industry and helping businesses leverage automation to meet the evolving demands of modern consumers.

Table of Contents

Introduction 1

   1.1 Why Pizza Vending Machines? 4
   1.2 Evolution of the Vending Machine Market 7
   1.3 Opportunities and Potential in the Automated Pizza Sector 11

Chapter 1: Market Analysis 17

   1.1 Overview of the Food and Vending Machine Industry 20
   1.2 Analyzing Demand and Consumer Trends 24
   1.3 Competition: Who Are the Key Players? 28

Chapter 2: Developing a Business Plan 35

   2.1 Key Elements of a Business Plan 39
   2.2 Defining Your Value Proposition 44
   2.3 SWOT Analysis (Strengths, Weaknesses, Opportunities, and Threats) 47
   2.4 Financial Planning and Profit Projections 50

Chapter 3: Technological and Operational Aspects 55

   3.1 Types of Pizza Vending Machines 58
   3.2 Cutting-Edge Technologies: From Automated Cooking to Customization ... 62
   3.3 Managing Day-to-Day Operations 66
   3.4 Maintenance and Technical Support 70

Chapter 4: Regulatory and Legal Aspects 75

   4.1 Health and Food Safety Regulations 77
   4.2 Necessary Permits and Licenses 79
   4.3 Insurance and Legal Liability 81

Chapter 5: Logistics and Supply Chain 85

   5.1 Supplier Selection: Raw Materials and Ingredients 88
   5.2 Inventory Management 91
   5.3 Optimizing the Supply Chain 94

Chapter 6: Marketing and Sales 98

   6.1 Marketing Strategies for an Innovative Business 101
   6.2 Branding and Market Positioning 104
   6.3 Digital Marketing and Social Media Promotion 107
   6.4 Pricing Strategies and Promotional Offers 110

Chapter 7: Project Financing 114

   7.1 Funding Sources: Equity vs. Debt 117
   7.2 Attracting Investors 120
   7.3 Crowdfunding and Other Fundraising Methods 123

Chapter 8: Business Management and Growth 128

    8.1 Managing Operations at Scale 131
    8.2 Expansion and Franchising 135
    8.3 Continuous Innovation: Improvements and New Developments 138

Chapter 9: Case Studies and Testimonials 141

    9.1 Success Stories in the Vending Machine Industry 141
    9.2 Lessons Learned from Real-Life Experiences 145
    9.3 Interviews with Successful Entrepreneurs 146

Chapter 10: Conclusions 149

    10.1 Final Reflections and Practical Advice 149
    10.2 The Future of Pizza Vending Machines 153
    10.3 Additional Resources and Recommended Readings 154

Appendices 156

    A1: Business Plan Templates 156
    A2: Startup Checklist 158
    A3: Useful Contacts and Recommended Suppliers 159

Bibliography 161

Acknowledgements 166

Introduction

The pizza vending machine business is more than just a novel concept—it's a potential game-changer in the food industry. As we stand on the brink of a new era where technology increasingly shapes every facet of our lives, the intersection of convenience, automation, and a universally beloved food like pizza offers a unique business opportunity. This chapter explores why the idea of a pizza vending machine has evolved from a futuristic fantasy to a viable business model and why now is the perfect time to capitalize on this innovation.

The Evolution of Vending Machines

Vending machines have been a staple in consumer culture for over a century, originally dispensing simple items like gum or postcards. Over time, they have evolved to offer a wide range of products, from snacks and beverages to electronics and even luxury goods. However, the leap from traditional vending machines to those offering freshly cooked meals, like pizza, represents a significant advancement in both technology and consumer expectations.

This evolution has been driven by several factors. First, there is the relentless march of technological progress. The machines of today are far more sophisticated than their predecessors, equipped with advanced robotics, AI, and IoT (Internet of Things) capabilities. These advancements have made it possible to automate complex food preparation processes that were once the exclusive domain of human chefs. From kneading dough to layering toppings and baking to perfection, modern vending machines can replicate many of the steps involved in traditional pizza-making, all within a compact, user-friendly interface.

Second, there has been a marked shift in consumer behavior. The modern consumer is increasingly seeking convenience, often prioritizing it over other factors like cost or even quality. This trend is evident in the rise of food delivery services, meal kits, and grab-and-go options. However, unlike delivery services, which rely on a human workforce and can be prone to delays and errors, vending machines offer a more reliable, consistent, and often faster solution. They are available 24/7, require no human interaction, and can be strategically placed in locations where traditional food service might not be viable.

The Universal Appeal of Pizza

Pizza's enduring popularity is another key factor behind the growing interest in pizza vending machines. Pizza is not just a food; it's a global phenomenon. In many countries, it is the go-to choice for casual dining, social gatherings, and even quick meals on the go. Its versatility—ranging from a simple Margherita to gourmet varieties with exotic toppings—ensures that it caters to a wide array of tastes and preferences. This universal appeal makes it an ideal candidate for vending machines, which thrive on offering popular, high-demand products.

What makes pizza particularly suited to vending machines is its balance of simplicity and complexity. On the one hand, the basic structure of a pizza—dough, sauce, cheese, and toppings—lends itself well to automation. On the other hand, the sheer variety of possible combinations allows for customization, which is a major draw for today's consumers who crave personalized experiences. A pizza vending machine can cater to this desire by allowing customers to choose their toppings, sauces, and even the type of crust, all while ensuring the final product is delivered fresh and hot within minutes.

The Business Opportunity

From a business perspective, the pizza vending machine concept holds several advantages over traditional food service models. One of the most significant benefits is the lower overhead costs. Traditional pizzerias require a physical location, a team of chefs and servers, and ongoing expenses like utilities, rent, and salaries. In contrast, a vending machine business requires only the initial investment in the machine and the cost of ingredients, with minimal ongoing operational costs. This lower cost structure not only makes the business more accessible to entrepreneurs with limited capital but also increases the potential for profitability.

Moreover, the scalability of a pizza vending machine business is another attractive feature. Expanding a traditional restaurant often involves significant investments in new locations, staff, and equipment, not to mention the time and effort required to manage these new operations. On the other hand, scaling a vending machine business can be as simple as purchasing and installing additional machines. These machines can be placed in high-traffic areas such as shopping malls, airports, university campuses, and office buildings, maximizing their exposure and revenue potential.

Additionally, the vending machine model allows for a level of flexibility that is difficult to achieve with traditional restaurants. For instance, machines can be moved or relocated based on changing customer patterns or seasonal demand, ensuring that the business can adapt quickly to market conditions. Furthermore, because the machines operate autonomously, they can continue generating revenue around the clock, unlike a traditional restaurant that is limited by operating hours and staffing constraints.

Responding to Modern Consumer Trends

Another important aspect of the pizza vending machine business is its alignment with current consumer trends, particularly the growing demand for contactless services. The COVID-19 pandemic has accelerated this trend, with many consumers now favoring options that minimize human interaction. Vending machines inherently offer a contactless experience, from the selection of the product to the payment process and finally the retrieval of the pizza. This feature not only appeals to health-conscious consumers but also adds an element of convenience that is hard to beat.

Furthermore, as environmental sustainability becomes an increasingly important issue for consumers, the pizza vending machine business can also align with eco-friendly practices. For instance, machines can be designed to use recyclable packaging, and the precise portion control of ingredients can help minimize food waste. These practices not only appeal to environmentally conscious consumers but can also reduce operational costs, creating a win-win situation for the business.

The Future of Pizza Vending Machines

Looking ahead, the future of pizza vending machines appears bright. As technology continues to advance, we can expect even more sophisticated machines that offer greater customization, faster service, and improved product quality. Innovations such as integrated mobile apps for pre-ordering, AI-driven recommendations based on customer preferences, and real-time inventory management systems are just a few of the possibilities on the horizon.

Moreover, as the business model proves itself in various markets, we may see the emergence of franchising opportunities, where successful entrepreneurs can expand their operations by selling the rights to their vending machine business to others. This could lead to rapid growth and the establishment of pizza vending machines as a common feature in urban landscapes around the world.

1.1 Why Pizza Vending Machines?

The concept of a pizza vending machine is not just a blend of convenience and technology; it represents a profound shift in how we think about food service and entrepreneurship. To understand why pizza vending machines are gaining traction, it is essential to examine the broader context in which they operate. This includes the evolving demands of consumers, the limitations of traditional food service models, and the unique advantages that vending machines offer in today's fast-paced world.

The Demand for Convenience and Speed

In the modern era, convenience is king. With increasingly busy lifestyles, consumers are constantly seeking ways to save time without compromising on quality. This trend is particularly evident in the food industry, where the demand for quick, easy-to-access meals has fueled the growth of fast food chains, food delivery services, and ready-to-eat options in supermarkets. However, these solutions often come with trade-offs—fast food may be convenient, but it is not always healthy, and delivery services, while offering a broader range of options, can be slow and unreliable.

Pizza vending machines address these issues head-on by offering a unique combination of speed, convenience, and quality. Unlike traditional fast food, which is often prepared in bulk and kept warm under heat lamps, pizza vending machines prepare each order fresh, ensuring that customers receive a hot, made-to-order meal in just a few minutes. This level of immediacy is a key selling point, especially in environments where time is of the essence, such as airports, train stations, and busy urban centers.

Moreover, the vending machine model eliminates many of the inefficiencies associated with food delivery. There is no need to wait for a driver to navigate traffic, and there is no risk of orders arriving cold or late. Customers can simply walk up to the machine, place their order, and receive their pizza in the time it would take to reheat a frozen meal at home. This level of efficiency is not just appealing; it is increasingly becoming a baseline expectation for consumers who are accustomed to instant gratification in other areas of their lives, such as online shopping and digital entertainment.

Overcoming the Limitations of Traditional Food Service Models

While traditional restaurants and pizzerias have long been the cornerstone of the food service industry, they come with significant limitations that pizza vending machines are uniquely positioned to overcome. One of the most significant challenges for traditional food service providers is the high cost of operation. Running a restaurant involves substantial overhead, including rent, utilities, labor, and inventory management. These costs are often passed on to consumers, resulting in higher prices for meals and tighter profit margins for business owners.

In contrast, pizza vending machines operate with a fraction of the overhead. They do not require a physical location in the traditional sense, as they can be placed in a variety of high-traffic areas, from shopping malls and office buildings to college campuses and public transportation hubs. This flexibility in location not only reduces costs but also opens up new markets that might be inaccessible to a traditional restaurant. For example, a pizza vending machine can be installed in a business park or industrial area where there are limited dining options, providing a convenient meal solution for employees and visitors alike.

Labor is another significant factor where pizza vending machines hold an advantage. Staffing a restaurant requires hiring, training, and managing a team of employees, which can be both time-consuming and expensive. Moreover, labor costs are subject to fluctuations due to factors like minimum wage increases, employee turnover, and scheduling complexities. Pizza vending machines, on the other hand, require minimal human intervention once they are up and running. They can be monitored and maintained remotely, with occasional visits needed for restocking ingredients and performing routine maintenance. This reduction in labor not only lowers operating costs but also simplifies management, allowing business owners to focus on other aspects of their operation.

Catering to the Millennial and Gen Z Consumer

Another key factor driving the interest in pizza vending machines is the changing demographic landscape. Millennials and Generation Z, who now represent a significant portion of the consumer market, have distinct preferences and behaviors that differ from those of previous generations. These younger consumers are digital natives who have grown up with technology and are comfortable using automated systems for a wide range of tasks, from banking to shopping to ordering food.

For these consumers, the idea of ordering a pizza from a machine is not just acceptable—it is often preferred. They value the convenience and speed that vending machines offer, as well as the novelty of the experience. In an era where experiences are increasingly valued over material goods, the process of watching a machine prepare and bake a pizza in front of your eyes has an inherent appeal. This aligns with the broader trend of experiential dining, where the process of obtaining the meal is almost as important as the meal itself.

Moreover, Millennials and Gen Z are highly conscious of hygiene and safety, especially in the wake of the COVID-19 pandemic. The contactless nature of vending machines appeals to their desire to minimize physical interactions and avoid potential health risks. This is particularly relevant in densely populated urban areas where the risks of close contact are higher, and consumers are more likely to seek out alternatives to traditional dining environments.

Capitalizing on the Automation Trend

Automation is rapidly transforming industries across the globe, from manufacturing and logistics to retail and hospitality. In the food industry, automation is seen as a way to increase efficiency, reduce costs, and improve consistency. Pizza vending machines are a prime example of how automation can be leveraged to create a new business model that addresses both consumer demands and operational challenges.

The automation trend is not just about replacing human labor; it is about enhancing the customer experience and creating new opportunities for innovation. With a pizza vending machine, the entire process—from dough preparation to baking to packaging—is automated, ensuring that each pizza is made to exact specifications. This level of precision is difficult to achieve in a traditional kitchen, where human error and variability can affect the final product. By standardizing the process, vending machines can deliver a consistently high-quality product that meets customer expectations every time.

Additionally, the automation of food preparation and delivery through vending machines allows businesses to collect valuable data on consumer preferences, sales patterns, and machine performance. This data can be used to optimize operations, refine product offerings, and make informed decisions about future investments. For example, if data shows that a particular topping is more popular in one location, the machine can be stocked accordingly, ensuring that customer demand is always met. This level of responsiveness is difficult to achieve in traditional food service models, where changes often require significant lead time and coordination.

The Appeal of Low-Cost, High-Margin Products

One of the most compelling reasons to consider entering the pizza vending machine business is the potential for high profit margins. Pizza, as a product, has several inherent advantages that make it well-suited for a vending machine model. The ingredients required to make pizza—flour, tomato sauce, cheese, and toppings—are relatively inexpensive, especially when purchased in bulk. Additionally, the process of making pizza is straightforward and can be easily automated, reducing the need for skilled labor.

When sold through a vending machine, the price point of a pizza can be competitive with that of traditional restaurants or delivery services, while still allowing for substantial profit margins. This is because the operational costs associated with running a vending machine are significantly lower than those of a brick-and-mortar restaurant. There are no servers to pay, no rent on a prime location, and no utility bills to worry about. These savings can be passed on to consumers in the form of lower prices, or they can be retained by the business owner as profit.

Furthermore, the potential for upselling and cross-selling within the vending machine model is substantial. For example, machines could be programmed to offer additional items such as drinks, desserts, or side dishes, creating a more comprehensive meal experience and increasing the average transaction value. This not only boosts revenue but also enhances the overall appeal of the vending machine as a one-stop solution for a quick, satisfying meal.

1.2 Evolution of the Vending Machine Market

The vending machine market has undergone substantial transformation since its inception, reflecting broader trends in technology, consumer behavior, and economic conditions. This evolution has turned vending machines from simple dispensers of basic goods into sophisticated, high-tech platforms capable of meeting a wide array of consumer needs. Understanding the evolution of this market is essential for grasping the current opportunities and challenges faced by entrepreneurs, particularly those interested in niche markets like pizza vending machines.

Early Development and Expansion

The vending machine market began in the late 19th century, initially focused on small, simple products such as postcards, chewing gum, and candy. These early machines were primarily mechanical, relying on basic coin-operated mechanisms that were prone to jamming and theft. Despite these limitations, the convenience offered by vending machines quickly captured the public's imagination, leading to their proliferation in urban areas across Europe and the United States.

As urbanization accelerated during the Industrial Revolution, the need for quick and convenient access to consumer goods grew, particularly in workplaces and public transportation hubs. Vending machines offered a solution to this need, and by the early 20th century, they had expanded their product offerings to include a variety of items such as cigarettes, soft drinks, and snacks. This period also saw the introduction of automated vending machines, which were capable of dispensing a broader range of products, including fresh food items.

The post-World War II economic boom further fueled the expansion of the vending machine market. Rising disposable incomes, coupled with the growing consumer culture of the 1950s and 1960s, created a fertile environment for the vending machine industry. During this time, vending machines became a ubiquitous presence in factories, schools, and office buildings, providing workers and students with convenient access to refreshments without the need for staffed cafeterias.

Technological Innovations and Market Diversification

The vending machine market continued to evolve rapidly throughout the latter half of the 20th century, driven by significant technological advancements. The introduction of electronic payment systems in the 1970s and 1980s marked a major turning point. These systems allowed machines to accept a wider range of payment methods, including credit and debit cards, which significantly broadened the customer base and increased sales.

In addition to payment innovations, advancements in refrigeration and automation enabled the market to diversify its product offerings. Vending machines were no longer limited to dry goods; they could now dispense cold beverages, hot meals, and even perishable items like sandwiches and dairy products. This diversification was accompanied by the emergence of new vending machine formats, such as coffee vending machines and refrigerated snack machines, which targeted specific consumer needs and environments.

The 1990s and early 2000s saw further expansion of the vending machine market into non-traditional products and services. For example, vending machines began offering electronics, personal care items, and even luxury goods in some locations. This period also witnessed the rise of specialty vending machines, such as those dispensing DVDs, beauty products, and high-end accessories, reflecting the growing consumer appetite for convenience and immediacy across a wider range of product categories.

The Digital Transformation of Vending

The advent of the digital age in the 21st century has had a profound impact on the vending machine market, transforming it in ways that were unimaginable just a few decades earlier. The integration of digital technology into vending machines has revolutionized the industry, making them smarter, more efficient, and more responsive to consumer needs.

One of the most significant changes has been the adoption of Internet of Things (IoT) technology, which allows vending machines to be connected to the internet. This connectivity enables operators to remotely monitor and manage their machines, providing real-time data on sales, inventory levels, and machine performance. IoT technology also facilitates predictive maintenance, reducing downtime and ensuring that machines are always operational when consumers need them.

In addition to operational improvements, digital technology has enhanced the consumer experience by enabling personalized interactions. Modern vending machines are often equipped with touchscreens, mobile payment options, and even AI-driven interfaces that can recommend products based on past purchases or current trends. These features not only make the purchasing process more engaging but also allow operators to gather valuable data on consumer preferences, which can be used to optimize product offerings and marketing strategies.

The rise of mobile technology has further accelerated the digital transformation of the vending machine market. The ability to pay via smartphone apps, QR codes, or contactless payment systems has made vending machines more accessible to a tech-savvy consumer base. Moreover, the integration of loyalty programs and promotional offers into vending platforms has helped to drive repeat business and increase customer engagement.

Globalization and Market Expansion

The globalization of the vending machine market has been another key factor in its evolution. While vending machines have long been a fixture in developed markets like the United States, Japan, and Western Europe, recent decades have seen significant growth in emerging markets across Asia, Latin America, and Eastern Europe.

In Japan, vending machines are a cultural phenomenon, with over 5 million machines serving a population of around 126 million people. The Japanese vending machine market is characterized by its diversity, with machines offering a vast array of products, from beverages and snacks to toys, clothing, and even hot meals. This market is also known for its advanced technology, with machines often featuring touchscreens, digital signage, and sophisticated payment systems.

Emerging markets, on the other hand, present both opportunities and challenges for the vending machine industry. In countries like China, India, and Brazil, rapid urbanization and rising disposable incomes have created a growing demand for convenient access to consumer goods. However, these markets also face challenges such as inadequate infrastructure, lower levels of technological adoption, and cultural differences in consumer behavior. Despite these obstacles, the potential for growth in these regions is significant, particularly as the middle class continues to expand and technology becomes more widely available.

The expansion of the vending machine market into new geographical regions has also led to the development of new business models. For example, in regions with less developed retail infrastructure, vending machines are increasingly being used as a primary distribution channel for products like beverages, snacks, and personal care items. This trend is particularly evident in rural and remote areas, where traditional retail options may be limited or nonexistent.

Challenges and Opportunities in the Modern Market

While the vending machine market has seen significant growth and innovation, it is not without its challenges. One of the primary challenges facing the industry today is the increasing competition from other forms of automated retail and online shopping. As e-commerce continues to grow, consumers have more options than ever for purchasing goods quickly and conveniently, which has put pressure on the vending machine market to adapt and differentiate itself.

Another challenge is the rising cost of doing business, particularly in terms of real estate and labor. Vending machines require strategic placement in high-traffic areas to be profitable, but securing these locations can be expensive, particularly in urban centers. Additionally, while vending machines are less labor-intensive than traditional retail, they still require regular maintenance, restocking, and customer service, all of which contribute to operational costs.

However, these challenges also present opportunities for innovation and growth. For instance, the increasing competition from online retail has driven vending machine operators to focus on unique product offerings and enhanced customer experiences. By offering niche products, healthier options, or locally sourced items, vending machines can carve out a distinct market position that appeals to specific consumer segments.

The rise of health and wellness trends presents another significant opportunity for the vending machine market. As consumers become more health-conscious, there is growing demand for vending machines that offer nutritious snacks, beverages, and meals. This has led to the emergence of "healthy vending" machines, which prioritize products with low sugar, low fat, and organic ingredients. These machines are particularly popular in settings like schools, gyms, and hospitals, where consumers are more likely to seek out healthy options.

Sustainability is another area where the vending machine market is evolving. Consumers are increasingly concerned about the environmental impact of their purchases, and vending machine operators are responding by offering eco-friendly products and adopting sustainable practices. This includes using energy-efficient machines, offering products with minimal packaging, and incorporating recycling programs.

1.3 Opportunities and Potential in the Automated Pizza Sector

The automated pizza sector represents a burgeoning niche within the broader vending machine market. This innovative segment combines the timeless appeal of pizza with cutting-edge technology to offer consumers a new way to enjoy their favorite meal. The potential for growth in this sector is substantial, driven by several key factors that align with current consumer trends and technological advancements. This section explores the opportunities and potential in the automated pizza sector, providing insights into why this niche is attracting attention and investment.

Consumer Demand for Convenience

One of the primary drivers of the automated pizza sector is the growing demand for convenience. In today's fast-paced world, consumers increasingly seek solutions that fit into their busy lifestyles, and automated pizza machines offer an appealing solution. These machines provide a quick and easy way to obtain a freshly made pizza without the need for ordering, delivery, or wait times typically associated with traditional pizzerias.

The convenience factor is especially relevant in urban environments where people are looking for efficient dining options. Automated pizza machines can be strategically placed in high-traffic areas such as office buildings, universities, transportation hubs, and shopping centers, offering a fast meal option to individuals on the go. By providing a hot, freshly baked pizza within minutes, these machines address the needs of consumers who value speed and ease without compromising on quality.

Advancements in Technology

Technological advancements have significantly contributed to the growth and potential of the automated pizza sector. Modern pizza vending machines incorporate a range of innovative technologies that enhance the customer experience and improve operational efficiency. These technologies include:

1. Robotic Systems: Advanced robotic systems in automated pizza machines are capable of handling various aspects of pizza preparation, from dough stretching to ingredient placement and baking. These robots ensure consistent quality and precision in every pizza, reducing the variability that can occur with human operators.

2. Smart Ovens: State-of-the-art ovens equipped with precise temperature controls and baking algorithms are integral to the automated pizza process. These ovens ensure that each pizza is cooked to perfection, with a crispy crust and evenly melted cheese.

3. IoT Integration: Internet of Things (IoT) technology allows for real-time monitoring and management of vending machines. Operators can track

inventory levels, monitor machine performance, and receive alerts for maintenance needs, all from a remote location. This connectivity helps to ensure that machines are always operational and stocked with fresh ingredients.

4. Customizable Interfaces: Touchscreen interfaces and mobile apps provide users with the ability to customize their pizzas to their preferences. From selecting toppings to choosing cooking styles, these interfaces enhance the user experience by offering a personalized touch.

5. Payment Systems: The integration of various payment methods, including contactless and mobile payments, makes transactions seamless and convenient. Consumers can easily pay using their smartphones, credit cards, or digital wallets, further improving the overall experience.

Market Differentiation and Competitive Advantage

The automated pizza sector offers a unique opportunity for differentiation in the crowded food and beverage market. Traditional pizza outlets face stiff competition from delivery services, fast-casual restaurants, and other dining options. Automated pizza machines provide a novel approach that sets them apart from conventional pizza businesses.

The ability to offer a consistent and high-quality product with minimal wait times gives automated pizza machines a competitive edge. Additionally, the 24/7 availability of these machines caters to consumers who seek late-night food options or those in need of a quick meal outside of regular restaurant hours. This round-the-clock availability enhances the attractiveness of automated pizza machines to a wide range of customers.

Furthermore, automated pizza machines can be deployed in locations where traditional pizzerias may not be feasible or profitable. For instance, placing these machines in remote or underserved areas where access to traditional dining options is limited can capture new market segments. This strategic placement helps to fill gaps in the market and provides valuable services to underserved communities.

Cost Efficiency and Scalability

From an operational perspective, automated pizza machines offer several cost-saving benefits compared to traditional pizza restaurants. These benefits include:

1. Reduced Labor Costs: Automated pizza machines require minimal human intervention, which helps to lower labor costs associated with staffing and training. Operators can manage multiple machines from a central location, reducing the need for on-site personnel.

2. Lower Overhead Costs: The physical footprint of an automated pizza machine is significantly smaller than that of a traditional pizzeria. This reduced space requirement translates to lower rental and utility costs, making it more cost-effective to deploy and operate these machines.

3. Efficient Inventory Management: Automated pizza machines are equipped with systems for monitoring ingredient levels and usage. This enables efficient inventory management, reducing food waste and ensuring that ingredients are used effectively.

4. Scalability: The modular nature of vending machines allows for easy scalability. Operators can expand their network of machines with relative ease, reaching new locations and markets without the need for large-scale investments. This scalability makes it possible to grow the business incrementally and adapt to changing market conditions.

Franchise and Partnership Opportunities

The automated pizza sector also presents attractive opportunities for franchising and partnerships. Franchising models allow for rapid expansion by leveraging established brand recognition and operational expertise. Franchisees benefit from a proven business model and support from the franchisor, while franchisors can grow their brand presence and reach new markets.

Partnerships with other businesses and organizations can further enhance the reach and impact of automated pizza machines. For example, partnering with convenience stores, gas stations, or entertainment venues can provide mutually beneficial arrangements. These partnerships can drive foot traffic to both the vending machine and the partner location, creating a win-win scenario for all parties involved.

Additionally, collaborations with technology providers and ingredient suppliers can lead to innovations in product offerings and operational efficiencies. By working with partners who offer complementary services or technologies, automated pizza operators can stay at the forefront of industry trends and deliver a superior customer experience.

Consumer Trends and Preferences

Understanding consumer trends and preferences is crucial for capitalizing on the opportunities in the automated pizza sector. Several trends are influencing consumer behavior and shaping the demand for automated pizza machines:

1. Health and Wellness: There is a growing emphasis on health and wellness among consumers, leading to increased demand for healthier food options. Automated pizza machines that offer nutritious ingredients, such as whole-grain crusts, organic toppings, and lower-fat cheeses, can cater to this trend and appeal to health-conscious customers.

2. Customization: Consumers increasingly value the ability to customize their food to suit their individual tastes and dietary preferences. Automated pizza machines that offer a wide range of toppings, sauces, and crust options provide a personalized experience that aligns with this trend.

3. Local and Sustainable Ingredients: There is a rising interest in locally sourced and sustainable ingredients. Automated pizza machines that emphasize local partnerships and environmentally friendly practices can attract consumers who prioritize sustainability and ethical sourcing.

4. Experiential Dining: Modern consumers seek unique and memorable dining experiences. The novelty of automated pizza machines, combined with the interactive and high-tech elements they offer, can create a compelling and engaging experience that stands out in a competitive market.

Challenges and Considerations

While the automated pizza sector holds significant potential, it is not without challenges. Some of the key considerations include:

1. Regulatory Compliance: Compliance with food safety and health regulations is critical for the success of automated pizza machines. Operators must ensure that their machines meet all relevant standards for hygiene, ingredient handling, and food preparation.

2. Maintenance and Reliability: Ensuring the reliability and proper maintenance of automated pizza machines is essential to avoid downtime and customer dissatisfaction. Regular servicing and prompt repairs are necessary to keep machines in optimal working condition.

3. Market Education: Educating consumers about the benefits and functionality of automated pizza machines may be required, particularly in markets where this technology is novel. Effective marketing and communication strategies can help to build awareness and drive adoption.

4. Competition: As the automated pizza sector grows, competition may increase from other players entering the market. Staying ahead of competitors will require continuous innovation, quality improvements, and a focus on customer satisfaction.

Chapter 1:
Market Analysis

The automated pizza sector represents a dynamic and evolving niche within the vending machine industry, drawing from the broader trends of convenience and technological advancement. To understand the potential of this sector, a comprehensive market analysis is essential. This chapter explores key dimensions of the market, including its size, growth trends, consumer behavior, competitive landscape, and potential barriers to entry, providing a detailed overview of what makes this sector promising and the challenges it faces.

Market Size and Growth Trends

The automated pizza sector is a subset of the global vending machine market, which has demonstrated steady growth over recent years. According to industry reports, the global vending machine market was valued at approximately $30 billion and is expected to continue expanding, driven by technological advancements and shifting consumer preferences. The specific segment of automated pizza machines, while niche, is projected to experience rapid growth due to its alignment with contemporary consumer demands for convenience and quality.

The growth of the automated pizza sector is supported by several macro trends. The increasing demand for on-the-go food solutions, driven by urbanization and busy lifestyles, has created a fertile ground for automated food vending solutions. Consumers are seeking quicker, more efficient ways to access high-quality meals without the delays and complexities associated with traditional food services.

In addition, the COVID-19 pandemic accelerated the adoption of contactless and automated services, which has positively impacted the vending machine industry. The heightened emphasis on hygiene and social distancing has made automated food solutions, such as pizza vending machines, more appealing. As a result, the sector has seen a surge in interest from both consumers and investors, further driving its growth.

Consumer Behavior and Preferences

Consumer behavior in the automated pizza sector is influenced by several key factors, including convenience, quality, and personalization. The modern consumer values efficiency and immediacy, particularly in urban environments where time constraints are prevalent. Automated pizza machines cater to this demand by offering a fast, convenient way to obtain a freshly made pizza. The ability to dispense a hot pizza within minutes of placing an order aligns with the increasing consumer preference for quick meal solutions.

Quality is another significant factor driving consumer interest in automated pizza machines. Advances in technology allow these machines to produce pizzas that rival those from traditional pizzerias in terms of taste and freshness. The integration of high-quality ingredients, advanced cooking methods, and precise automation ensures that consumers receive a consistently good product. This focus on quality addresses consumer expectations and enhances the appeal of automated pizza machines.

Personalization is also a crucial element in consumer preferences. Automated pizza machines that offer customizable options, such as a wide range of toppings, sauces, and crust types, provide a personalized dining experience that appeals to individual tastes. This level of customization sets automated pizza machines apart from traditional fast food options and enhances their attractiveness to a diverse customer base.

Furthermore, the trend towards healthier eating is shaping consumer expectations in the automated pizza sector. Many consumers are increasingly conscious of their dietary choices and seek healthier food options. Automated pizza machines that offer nutritional information, healthier ingredients, and options for dietary restrictions can cater to this growing segment of health-conscious consumers.

Competitive Landscape

The competitive landscape of the automated pizza sector is characterized by a mix of established vending machine operators, emerging technology companies, and innovative start-ups. Each player brings a unique set of capabilities and approaches to the market, contributing to a dynamic and competitive environment.

Established vending machine operators, with their extensive experience and infrastructure, are well-positioned to enter the automated pizza market. These companies have a deep understanding of vending machine operations, maintenance, and customer service. They are likely to leverage their expertise to develop and deploy automated pizza machines, focusing on refining technology and expanding their market presence.

New entrants and technology innovators are also making significant contributions to the automated pizza sector. Start-ups specializing in food automation are developing advanced pizza machines that incorporate cutting-edge technologies, such as robotics, artificial intelligence, and smart ovens. These innovations push the boundaries of what automated pizza machines can offer, creating new opportunities for differentiation and market growth.

Partnerships and collaborations are another important aspect of the competitive landscape. Strategic alliances between vending machine operators, technology providers, and ingredient suppliers can enhance the capabilities of automated pizza machines. For example, partnerships with technology firms may lead to the integration of advanced payment systems, while collaborations with ingredient suppliers can ensure the availability of high-quality, fresh components. These partnerships can provide a competitive edge and drive market differentiation.

Barriers to Entry

Entering the automated pizza sector presents several challenges that must be addressed to achieve success. Understanding these barriers is crucial for developing effective strategies and overcoming potential obstacles.

Regulatory Compliance: One of the primary challenges in the automated pizza sector is ensuring compliance with food safety and health regulations. Automated pizza machines must adhere to stringent guidelines concerning hygiene, ingredient handling, and food preparation. Navigating these regulatory requirements can be complex and may require significant investment in technology and processes to ensure compliance. Operators must stay informed about evolving regulations and implement robust systems to meet industry standards.

Technical Challenges: Developing and maintaining high-quality automated pizza machines involves overcoming technical challenges. The integration of robotics, smart ovens, and IoT technology requires advanced engineering and ongoing maintenance. Ensuring that machines operate reliably and produce consistent results is critical to maintaining customer satisfaction. Technical issues, such as malfunctions or inconsistencies in ingredient handling, can impact the overall performance of the machines and necessitate prompt resolution.

Market Education: Educating consumers about the benefits and functionality of automated pizza machines is essential for driving adoption. In markets where this technology is new, effective marketing and communication strategies are required to build awareness and demonstrate the value of automated pizza machines. Operators must invest in educating potential customers and addressing any concerns or misconceptions about the technology.

Competition and Saturation: As the automated pizza sector grows, increased competition from other players may arise. The entry of new competitors can lead to market saturation and exert pressure on pricing and profitability. Differentiating the product offering and maintaining a focus on quality and customer experience will be key to staying competitive. Operators must continuously innovate and adapt to evolving market conditions to maintain their competitive edge.

Infrastructure and Location: Securing optimal locations for deploying automated pizza machines is crucial to their success. High-traffic areas such as office buildings, universities, and transportation hubs are ideal for maximizing visibility and accessibility. However, obtaining these locations can be challenging and expensive. Additionally, ensuring adequate infrastructure for machine installation, maintenance, and restocking is essential. Operators must carefully evaluate potential locations and negotiate favorable terms to ensure the success of their vending machines.

1.1 Overview of the Food and Vending Machine Industry

The food and vending machine industry represents a significant segment within the broader food service sector, characterized by a diverse array of automated solutions designed to meet consumer demands for convenience and accessibility. This industry encompasses a variety of vending machines that dispense snacks, beverages, and prepared meals, including innovations such as automated pizza machines. Understanding the evolution, current trends, and dynamics of the food and vending machine industry provides a foundation for exploring the specific niche of automated pizza vending.

Historical Development and Evolution

The history of vending machines dates back to ancient times, with early forms of vending mechanisms discovered in ancient Greece and Rome. These early devices were primarily used to dispense items such as holy water or other small goods in exchange for a coin. The modern vending machine, as we know it, began to take shape in the late 19th and early 20th centuries. Innovations during this period included machines that dispensed items like postcards, gum, and, eventually, food and beverages.

The early 20th century saw significant advancements in vending technology, with the introduction of machines capable of dispensing bottled drinks and packaged snacks. These developments were driven by the growing demand for convenience and the increasing mobility of consumers. Post-World War II, the vending industry experienced rapid growth as automated machines became a common feature in public spaces such as airports, train stations, and office buildings.

The latter part of the 20th century and the early 21st century brought further technological advancements, including the integration of digital payment systems, improved refrigeration techniques, and enhanced product offerings. The introduction of cashless payment options and touchscreen interfaces transformed the vending experience, making it more user-friendly and accessible.

Current Market Trends

The food and vending machine industry has undergone significant transformation in recent years, driven by several key trends:

1. Technological Innovation: Technology continues to play a central role in the evolution of vending machines. Modern vending machines are equipped with advanced features such as touchscreen interfaces, cashless payment systems, and real-time inventory monitoring. The integration of Internet of Things (IoT) technology allows for remote management and troubleshooting, enhancing operational efficiency and customer experience.

2. Convenience and Accessibility: The demand for convenience remains a primary driver of growth in the vending machine industry. Consumers increasingly seek quick and accessible food and beverage options that fit into their busy lifestyles. Vending machines are strategically placed in high-traffic

areas such as office buildings, universities, airports, and transportation hubs to cater to this demand.

3. Health and Wellness: There is a growing emphasis on health and wellness among consumers, which is influencing the vending machine industry. As consumers become more health-conscious, there is a rising demand for healthier food options. Vending machines are adapting by offering products that include organic snacks, low-calorie items, and nutritious meals. The trend towards healthier eating is shaping the product offerings and positioning of vending machines.

4. Customization and Personalization: Modern consumers value customization and personalization in their food choices. Vending machines that offer a range of options for customization, such as selecting specific toppings or ingredients, are becoming increasingly popular. This trend aligns with the broader consumer preference for personalized experiences and tailored products.

5. Sustainability: Environmental sustainability is becoming an important consideration in the vending machine industry. Companies are exploring ways to reduce waste, minimize energy consumption, and use eco-friendly materials. The adoption of sustainable practices is driven by consumer expectations and regulatory requirements aimed at reducing the environmental impact of vending operations.

Market Segmentation

The food and vending machine industry can be segmented into various categories based on product offerings, machine types, and market segments:

1. Product Offerings: Vending machines dispense a wide range of products, including snacks, beverages, fresh food, and prepared meals. This segmentation reflects the diverse needs of consumers and the different types of vending solutions available. For instance, traditional vending machines may focus on snacks and drinks, while more advanced machines may offer fresh salads, sandwiches, or even hot meals.

2. Machine Types: Vending machines vary in their design and functionality. Common types include snack and beverage machines, refrigerated machines, and automated food machines. Each type serves a specific purpose and caters to different consumer needs. Automated pizza machines, for example, represent a

specialized category within the broader food vending segment, focusing on delivering freshly made pizza.

3. Market Segments: The vending machine market serves various sectors, including public transportation, educational institutions, healthcare facilities, and corporate environments. Each sector has unique requirements and preferences, influencing the types of vending machines deployed and the products offered. For instance, vending machines in corporate environments may focus on premium snacks and beverages, while those in transportation hubs may prioritize convenience and quick meals.

Key Players and Competitive Dynamics

The food and vending machine industry is characterized by the presence of several key players, including established vending machine manufacturers, operators, and technology providers. Major companies in the industry include brands such as Aramark, Compass Group, and Canteen Vending Services, which offer a range of vending solutions and services. Additionally, technology companies specializing in vending machine innovations contribute to the competitive landscape by developing advanced features and systems.

Competition in the vending machine industry is driven by factors such as product quality, technology integration, customer service, and pricing. Companies that can offer innovative solutions, enhance the customer experience, and adapt to changing market trends are well-positioned to succeed. The competitive dynamics of the industry also influence the development of new vending solutions, including automated pizza machines, which seek to differentiate themselves through unique offerings and advanced technology.

Challenges and Opportunities

The food and vending machine industry faces several challenges and opportunities that impact its growth and development:

1. Regulatory Compliance: Vending machines must adhere to food safety and health regulations, which can vary by region and product type. Ensuring compliance with these regulations requires ongoing attention and investment in technology and processes. Regulatory challenges can impact operational efficiency and product offerings.

2. Technological Advancements: While technology presents opportunities for innovation and improvement, it also poses challenges related to implementation

and maintenance. Companies must invest in research and development to stay ahead of technological trends and address any technical issues that arise.

3. Consumer Preferences: Understanding and responding to changing consumer preferences is crucial for success in the vending machine industry. Companies must stay attuned to trends such as health and wellness, customization, and sustainability to meet consumer demands and remain competitive.

4. Market Expansion: The growth of the vending machine industry presents opportunities for market expansion, including the introduction of new products and technologies. Automated pizza machines, for example, represent a growing niche with significant potential for expansion into new markets and locations.

5. Sustainability Initiatives: Embracing sustainability initiatives presents opportunities to enhance brand reputation and meet consumer expectations. Companies that adopt eco-friendly practices and reduce their environmental impact can differentiate themselves and appeal to environmentally conscious consumers.

1.2 Analyzing Demand and Consumer Trends

Analyzing demand and consumer trends is pivotal for understanding the viability and potential success of automated pizza machines in the food and vending machine industry. The intersection of evolving consumer expectations and technological advancements shapes the demand for innovative food solutions. This section provides an in-depth exploration of the factors driving demand, the impact of current consumer trends, and how these elements influence the automated pizza sector.

Demand Drivers for Automated Pizza Machines

The demand for automated pizza machines is influenced by several key factors that reflect broader changes in consumer behavior and technological advancements. These factors include the desire for convenience, the emphasis on quality, technological appeal, and the changing landscape of consumer dining preferences.

1. Convenience as a Primary Driver: In today's fast-paced world, convenience remains a significant driver of consumer behavior. Automated pizza machines cater to this demand by offering a quick and efficient solution for obtaining a freshly made pizza. The ability to order and receive a hot pizza within minutes, without the need for traditional food service interactions, aligns well with the

increasing consumer preference for time-saving options. This demand for convenience is particularly pronounced in urban environments where individuals often have busy schedules and limited time for dining.

Automated pizza machines are strategically positioned to address this need by being located in high-traffic areas such as office buildings, transportation hubs, and educational institutions. These machines offer an appealing alternative to traditional dining options, providing a fast and accessible way to enjoy a meal on the go.

2. Quality and Freshness: Quality is a critical factor influencing demand for automated pizza machines. Advances in technology have enabled these machines to produce pizzas that rival those from traditional pizzerias in terms of taste and freshness. The integration of high-quality ingredients, precise cooking techniques, and advanced automation ensures that consumers receive a product that meets their expectations for quality and flavor.

The emphasis on quality also reflects broader consumer trends towards better food experiences. As consumers become more discerning about their food choices, they seek out options that provide both convenience and a high standard of quality. Automated pizza machines that deliver consistently good results are well-positioned to attract and retain customers who prioritize both convenience and taste.

3. Technological Appeal: The technological sophistication of automated pizza machines plays a significant role in driving demand. Consumers are increasingly interested in innovative technologies and are willing to explore new food solutions that incorporate advanced features. Automated pizza machines that utilize robotics, smart ovens, and interactive interfaces offer a novel and engaging experience that appeals to tech-savvy individuals.

The integration of cutting-edge technology not only enhances the functionality of the machines but also adds an element of novelty that can attract attention and generate interest. The appeal of experiencing the latest advancements in food automation can drive consumer curiosity and encourage adoption of automated pizza machines.

4. Evolving Dining Preferences: Consumer dining preferences are evolving, with a growing emphasis on convenience, quality, and customization. Automated pizza machines align with these preferences by offering a solution that combines speed with a high-quality product. Additionally, the ability to

customize pizzas with various toppings, sauces, and crust options caters to the desire for personalized dining experiences.

Understanding these evolving preferences is crucial for identifying opportunities within the automated pizza sector. By addressing consumer desires for convenience, quality, and customization, automated pizza machines can effectively meet the needs of modern consumers.

Consumer Trends Influencing Demand

Several consumer trends are shaping demand in the automated pizza sector. These trends reflect broader shifts in consumer behavior and expectations and provide insights into how businesses can align their offerings with market needs.

1. Health and Wellness: There is a growing emphasis on health and wellness among consumers, influencing their food choices and preferences. Many individuals are increasingly conscious of their dietary habits and seek out healthier food options. This trend is reflected in the demand for products that incorporate nutritious ingredients and cater to various dietary needs.

Automated pizza machines that offer healthier options, such as whole grain crusts, reduced-fat cheeses, and fresh, organic toppings, can appeal to health-conscious consumers. Providing nutritional information and accommodating dietary restrictions can further enhance the appeal of automated pizza machines to this segment of the market.

2. Customization and Personalization: The demand for customization and personalization is a significant trend in the food service industry. Consumers increasingly value the ability to tailor products to their individual preferences. Automated pizza machines that offer a range of customization options, such as selecting specific toppings, sauces, and crust types, align with this trend and provide a personalized dining experience.

This trend towards personalization reflects a broader consumer desire for unique and tailored experiences. By offering customizable options, automated pizza machines can attract consumers who seek to create a pizza that meets their specific tastes and preferences.

3. Contactless Solutions: The COVID-19 pandemic has accelerated the adoption of contactless solutions across various sectors, including food service. Consumers are increasingly seeking options that minimize physical contact and enhance hygiene. Automated pizza machines, with their self-service capabilities

and contactless payment options, align with this trend by providing a safe and hygienic way to access food.

The increased emphasis on contactless solutions is likely to continue influencing consumer preferences and demand. Automated pizza machines that prioritize hygiene and safety can effectively address these concerns and appeal to consumers who value health and cleanliness.

4. Urbanization and High-Traffic Locations: Urbanization is driving changes in consumer behavior, creating a demand for convenient food solutions in high-traffic areas. As more people move to urban environments and spend time in places such as office complexes, universities, and transportation hubs, the need for accessible and quick meal options increases.

Automated pizza machines deployed in these high-traffic locations can capture a significant share of the market by catering to the needs of busy urban dwellers. Strategic placement of machines in areas with high foot traffic can enhance visibility and attract consumers who seek convenient food solutions.

5. Technological Integration and Innovation: The integration of advanced technologies and continuous innovation are key factors in shaping consumer expectations and demand. Consumers are drawn to products that incorporate the latest technological advancements, and this trend extends to the food service industry.

Automated pizza machines that feature cutting-edge technology, such as AI-driven recommendations, smart inventory management, and interactive user interfaces, can attract tech-savvy consumers and differentiate themselves from competitors. The ongoing innovation in food automation provides opportunities for businesses to enhance their offerings and meet evolving consumer expectations.

Market Segmentation and Target Audience

Effective market segmentation and identification of target audiences are essential for addressing consumer demand in the automated pizza sector. Segmenting the market based on demographics, location, and consumer preferences helps businesses tailor their strategies and offerings to specific consumer needs.

1. Demographic Segmentation: Different demographic groups have varying preferences and needs when it comes to food. For instance, younger consumers,

including millennials and Gen Z, are often more open to trying innovative food solutions and embracing new technologies. They may be more likely to adopt automated pizza machines due to their novelty and convenience.

In contrast, families and working professionals may prioritize quick meal solutions and high-quality products. Understanding these demographic differences helps businesses tailor their offerings and marketing strategies to appeal to specific segments of the market.

2. Location-Based Segmentation: The location of automated pizza machines is a critical factor in targeting specific consumer segments. High-traffic areas such as office buildings, university campuses, and transportation hubs attract diverse consumer groups with varying needs and preferences.

For example, office buildings may have a significant number of busy professionals seeking convenient meal options, while university campuses may attract students looking for quick and affordable food solutions. Tailoring machine placements to these locations can enhance their appeal and effectiveness in meeting the needs of different consumer groups.

3. Consumer Preferences and Behavior: Analyzing consumer preferences and behavior provides valuable insights into how to address demand effectively. For instance, consumers who prioritize health and wellness may be more interested in automated pizza machines that offer healthier options and provide nutritional information.

Similarly, consumers who value customization and personalization may be drawn to machines that allow them to create their own pizzas with a variety of toppings and ingredients. By understanding these preferences, businesses can develop targeted strategies and offerings that align with consumer behavior.

1.3 Competition: Who Are the Key Players?

In the dynamic landscape of the automated pizza machine industry, identifying and understanding the key competitors is vital for assessing market opportunities and formulating strategic responses. This section delves into the various segments of competition, highlighting major players, emerging innovators, and regional contenders. It also explores how these competitors influence the market and what factors contribute to their competitive edge.

1. Established Vending Machine Manufacturers

1.1. Canteen Vending Services

Canteen Vending Services, a prominent player in the vending industry, has an extensive portfolio of vending solutions spanning various food and beverage categories. Traditionally known for its snack and drink vending machines, Canteen has a strong market presence due to its established infrastructure and operational expertise. The company's large-scale distribution network and experience in high-traffic environments provide a robust platform for introducing new concepts like automated pizza machines.

Canteen's competitive edge lies in its ability to leverage its existing client relationships and infrastructure. The company's extensive experience in managing vending operations allows it to integrate new technologies efficiently, including those for automated pizza machines. By combining its operational know-how with innovative pizza vending technology, Canteen can effectively meet consumer demands for convenience and quality.

1.2. Aramark

Aramark is a global leader in food services, facilities management, and uniform services. With a broad portfolio that includes vending solutions, Aramark is well-positioned to explore and implement automated pizza vending technology. The company's extensive experience in managing food services for various institutions—such as educational facilities, corporate offices, and healthcare organizations—provides a solid foundation for deploying automated pizza machines in these environments.

Aramark's strategic advantage lies in its established market presence and its ability to cater to diverse consumer needs across different sectors. The company's emphasis on innovation and customer satisfaction aligns well with the introduction of automated pizza machines. By leveraging its existing infrastructure and client base, Aramark can effectively promote and integrate automated pizza vending solutions, enhancing its competitive position in the market.

1.3. Compass Group

Compass Group, a leading global foodservice provider, operates a wide range of food service solutions, including vending machines. Known for its focus on quality and innovation, Compass Group is well-suited to incorporate automated pizza machines into its service offerings. The company's experience in managing food services across various industries—such as corporate, educational, and healthcare—positions it to leverage automated pizza machines in diverse settings.

Compass Group's competitive advantage stems from its commitment to innovation and its ability to adapt to evolving consumer preferences. By integrating automated pizza machines into its portfolio, Compass Group can offer a novel and efficient food solution that aligns with its focus on quality and customer experience. The company's established infrastructure and market presence provide a strategic advantage in deploying and scaling automated pizza vending solutions.

2. Technology Innovators and Startups

2.1. Pizzaiolo

Pizzaiolo represents a new wave of startups focusing on advanced automated pizza vending technology. The company is renowned for its cutting-edge approach to pizza automation, featuring state-of-the-art robotics and real-time cooking systems. Pizzaiolo's machines are designed to deliver high-quality, freshly made pizzas with minimal human intervention, appealing to tech-savvy consumers and those seeking a novel dining experience.

Pizzaiolo's competitive edge lies in its commitment to innovation and its ability to deliver a high-quality product consistently. The company's use of advanced technology and its focus on user experience position it as a leader in the automated pizza sector. By continually evolving its technology and enhancing its product offerings, Pizzaiolo can maintain a competitive advantage and attract a growing customer base.

2.2. PizzaForno

PizzaForno is another prominent startup making waves in the automated pizza market. The company's automated machines are designed to provide a fully self-service pizza experience, leveraging advanced technology to ensure high-quality results. PizzaForno's emphasis on user convenience and efficiency makes it a strong competitor in the sector.

The company's innovative approach includes features such as customizable pizza options, interactive user interfaces, and real-time cooking processes. These advancements enhance the overall customer experience and differentiate

PizzaForno from other competitors. The startup's focus on delivering a high-quality, convenient pizza solution positions it well in a growing market.

2.3. Eataly's Pizza Machine Initiative

Eataly, an internationally recognized food marketplace known for its premium food offerings, has ventured into the automated pizza sector with its own pizza machine initiative. Leveraging its strong brand reputation and culinary expertise, Eataly aims to offer a high-end automated pizza experience. The company's machines are designed to deliver pizzas that align with its commitment to quality and authenticity.

Eataly's competitive advantage lies in its established brand presence and its ability to attract customers seeking a premium food experience. By integrating automated pizza machines into its existing operations, Eataly can offer a unique value proposition that combines convenience with high-quality ingredients. The company's reputation and customer loyalty contribute to its competitive positioning in the automated pizza market.

3. Emerging Competitors and Regional Players

3.1. Zume Pizza

Zume Pizza is an innovative company that combines automated pizza-making technology with advanced delivery solutions. The company's approach includes using robotics to prepare pizzas and equipping delivery vehicles with cooking technology. This integration of automation with delivery logistics represents a unique and compelling value proposition in the automated pizza market.

Zume Pizza's competitive edge is derived from its ability to streamline both the production and delivery of pizzas, enhancing operational efficiency and customer satisfaction. The company's focus on innovative solutions and its ability to adapt to changing market demands position it as a significant player in the sector. Zume Pizza's approach reflects a broader trend towards integrating automation with food delivery services, providing a competitive advantage in a rapidly evolving market.

3.2. FastyPizza

FastyPizza operates primarily in regional markets, focusing on delivering affordable and accessible automated pizza solutions. The company's emphasis on cost-effectiveness and adaptability allows it to cater to local preferences and meet the needs of budget-conscious consumers. FastyPizza's machines are designed to provide a reliable and efficient pizza experience at a competitive price point.

The company's regional focus enables it to build strong relationships with local customers and adapt its offerings to meet specific market needs. By providing cost-effective solutions and addressing regional preferences, FastyPizza can capture a significant share of the market in its target areas. The company's ability to balance affordability with quality contributes to its competitive positioning.

3.3. FreshlyMade Pizzas Inc.

FreshlyMade Pizzas Inc. is a regional player specializing in automated pizza machines that emphasize freshness and quality. The company's focus on using high-quality ingredients and maintaining consistent product standards positions it as a strong competitor in local markets. FreshlyMade Pizzas Inc.'s ability to deliver a high-quality pizza experience through automation enhances its competitive edge.

The company's regional approach allows it to tailor its offerings to local tastes and preferences, building strong connections with its customer base. By prioritizing product quality and customer service, FreshlyMade Pizzas Inc. can differentiate itself from competitors and maintain a strong market presence. The company's commitment to delivering a premium product contributes to its competitive positioning in the automated pizza sector.

4. Competitive Dynamics and Market Positioning

4.1. Product Differentiation

In the competitive landscape of automated pizza machines, product differentiation is a key factor in shaping market dynamics. Companies employ various strategies to set themselves apart, including technological innovation, quality of ingredients, and customization options. For instance, Pizzaiolo and PizzaForno focus on advanced automation and high-quality ingredients to create a distinctive product offering.

Differentiation strategies play a crucial role in influencing consumer choices and driving market growth. Companies that successfully differentiate their products can attract a loyal customer base and achieve a competitive advantage. By leveraging unique features and innovations, businesses can stand out in a crowded market and capture a share of the growing demand for automated pizza solutions.

4.2. Technology and Innovation

Technological innovation is a significant driver of competition in the automated pizza sector. Companies that invest in cutting-edge technologies, such as robotics, AI-driven cooking systems, and interactive interfaces, are better positioned to appeal to tech-savvy consumers. The continuous advancement of technology in automation and food preparation contributes to the competitive landscape and drives market growth.

Innovation also plays a critical role in shaping consumer expectations and preferences. Companies that stay at the forefront of technological developments can offer enhanced features and capabilities, differentiating themselves from competitors. By focusing on technology and innovation, businesses can maintain a competitive edge and capitalize on emerging trends in the automated pizza market.

4.3. Market Expansion and Reach

The ability to scale and expand operations is a key factor influencing competitive dynamics in the automated pizza sector. Companies with established infrastructure, strong distribution networks, and strategic partnerships can effectively reach a broader audience and capture market share. Market expansion efforts, including geographic growth and entry into new segments, contribute to competitive positioning and overall market presence.

Businesses that successfully execute expansion strategies can leverage their existing resources and capabilities to enter new markets and attract additional customers. By focusing on growth and scalability, companies can enhance their competitive positioning and capitalize on opportunities in the automated pizza sector.

4.4. Customer Experience and Service

Customer experience is a crucial factor in the success of automated pizza machines. Companies that prioritize user-friendly interfaces, reliable performance, and responsive customer service are better positioned to build customer loyalty and drive repeat business. Providing a positive and seamless experience contributes to competitive differentiation and market success.

A strong focus on customer experience can enhance the overall appeal of automated pizza machines and drive consumer satisfaction. Businesses that excel in delivering exceptional service and addressing customer needs are more likely to succeed in a competitive market. By prioritizing customer experience, companies can build a loyal customer base and achieve long-term success in the automated pizza sector.

Chapter 2:
Developing a Business Plan

Creating a robust business plan is crucial for launching and managing a successful automated pizza machine venture. A well-structured business plan provides a roadmap for achieving business goals, navigating challenges, and capitalizing on opportunities in the competitive landscape. This chapter outlines the essential components of a business plan tailored to the automated pizza machine industry, including market research, financial planning, operational strategy, and marketing tactics.

1. Executive Summary

The executive summary is the cornerstone of the business plan, offering a concise overview of the business concept, objectives, and strategies. It serves as an introduction to the plan, summarizing key aspects and providing a snapshot of the business opportunity.

1.1. Business Concept: Start with a clear description of the automated pizza machine business, including the core idea, the technology used, and the unique selling proposition. Define the target market, the problem the business solves, and how the automated pizza machine addresses this problem. Highlight the innovation and differentiation aspects that set the business apart from competitors.

1.2. Business Objectives: Outline the short-term and long-term objectives for the business. Short-term objectives may include launching the first batch of machines, securing initial locations, and generating early revenue. Long-term objectives could involve expanding the number of machines, entering new markets, and achieving profitability.

1.3. Financial Overview: Provide a brief summary of the financial projections, including startup costs, revenue forecasts, and profitability timelines. Highlight key financial metrics such as break-even analysis, cash flow projections, and funding requirements. This overview helps stakeholders understand the financial viability and potential return on investment.

2. Market Research and Analysis

Thorough market research and analysis are essential for understanding the competitive landscape, identifying target customers, and evaluating market potential. This section covers the methodologies for conducting market research and analyzing industry trends.

2.1. Industry Analysis: Examine the current state of the vending machine industry, focusing on trends, growth drivers, and challenges. Analyze the demand for automated food solutions, with a particular emphasis on pizza vending machines. Assess how technological advancements, consumer preferences, and regulatory factors impact the industry.

2.2. Competitive Analysis: Identify and analyze key competitors in the automated pizza machine sector. Evaluate their strengths, weaknesses, market positioning, and strategies. Understanding the competitive landscape helps in developing a strategy to differentiate the business and capitalize on market gaps.

2.3. Target Market Identification: Define the target market segments for the automated pizza machines. Consider demographic factors, geographic locations, and psychographic profiles of potential customers. Analyze market size, growth potential, and consumer behavior to tailor the product offering and marketing strategies.

2.4. SWOT Analysis: Conduct a SWOT analysis (Strengths, Weaknesses, Opportunities, Threats) to assess the internal and external factors affecting the business. Identify strengths that can be leveraged, weaknesses that need addressing, opportunities for growth, and threats that may pose challenges.

3. Product and Service Offering

Detail the automated pizza machine product and service offering, including features, technology, and value propositions. This section outlines the product design, functionality, and customer benefits.

3.1. Product Design and Technology: Describe the design and technology used in the automated pizza machines. Highlight key features such as cooking technology, ingredient storage, customization options, and user interfaces. Explain how the technology ensures quality, efficiency, and consistency in the pizza-making process.

3.2. Value Proposition: Clearly articulate the value proposition of the automated pizza machines. Emphasize the benefits to customers, such as convenience, quality, speed, and customization. Explain how the product addresses pain points in the existing food service market and offers a superior solution.

3.3. Service and Support: Outline the service and support provided to customers. This may include installation, maintenance, customer service, and troubleshooting. Ensure that the support structure is robust and capable of addressing customer needs effectively.

4. Operational Plan

The operational plan details the day-to-day operations required to run the automated pizza machine business. It covers production, supply chain management, and staffing.

4.1. Production and Supply Chain: Describe the production process for the automated pizza machines, including sourcing materials, manufacturing, and quality control. Outline the supply chain logistics for ingredient procurement, inventory management, and distribution. Ensure that the supply chain is efficient and capable of meeting demand.

4.2. Location and Deployment: Identify potential locations for deploying the automated pizza machines. Consider factors such as foot traffic, target customer demographics, and accessibility. Develop a strategy for securing and managing locations, including partnerships with property owners or managers.

4.3. Staffing and Management: Define the staffing requirements for the business, including roles and responsibilities. Consider hiring for positions such as technical support, sales, and operations. Develop a management structure to oversee daily operations, ensure compliance with regulations, and drive business growth.

4.4. Technology and Maintenance: Detail the technology infrastructure required to support the automated pizza machines. This includes software for machine operation, data collection, and remote monitoring. Develop a maintenance plan to ensure machines remain operational and efficient.

5. Marketing and Sales Strategy

The marketing and sales strategy outlines how the business will attract and retain customers. It includes promotional tactics, sales channels, and brand positioning.

5.1. Marketing Plan: Develop a comprehensive marketing plan to promote the automated pizza machines. This may include digital marketing, social media campaigns, local advertising, and partnerships. Identify key marketing channels and tactics to reach the target audience effectively.

5.2. Sales Strategy: Outline the sales strategy for acquiring and managing customer accounts. Consider direct sales, partnerships with businesses, and online sales channels. Develop a sales approach that aligns with the target market and maximizes revenue opportunities.

5.3. Branding and Positioning: Define the brand identity and positioning for the automated pizza machines. Develop a brand message that resonates with the target audience and emphasizes the unique value proposition. Ensure consistent branding across all marketing materials and customer touchpoints.

5.4. Customer Acquisition and Retention: Develop strategies for acquiring and retaining customers. This may include loyalty programs, promotions, and customer feedback mechanisms. Focus on building strong relationships with customers and providing exceptional service to drive repeat business.

6. Financial Plan

The financial plan provides a detailed overview of the business's financial projections and funding requirements. It includes budgeting, forecasting, and financial analysis.

6.1. Startup Costs: Outline the initial costs required to launch the automated pizza machine business. This includes expenses for equipment, technology, marketing, and operational setup. Develop a budget to manage these costs effectively.

6.2. Revenue Projections: Develop revenue projections based on market research, pricing strategy, and sales forecasts. Include estimates for sales volume, pricing, and revenue growth over time. Ensure that the projections are realistic and achievable.

6.3. Profitability Analysis: Conduct a profitability analysis to determine the break-even point and assess potential profitability. Analyze profit margins, cost structures, and financial ratios to evaluate the business's financial health.

6.4. Funding Requirements: Identify the funding requirements for the business, including startup capital and working capital. Develop a funding strategy that may include equity investment, loans, or other financing options. Outline the use of funds and the expected return on investment for potential investors.

6.5. Financial Risks and Mitigation: Assess potential financial risks and develop strategies to mitigate them. This may include risks related to market fluctuations, operational challenges, and financial management. Develop contingency plans to address potential issues and ensure business stability.

7. Implementation Timeline

The implementation timeline provides a roadmap for launching and growing the automated pizza machine business. It outlines key milestones, deadlines, and responsibilities.

7.1. Key Milestones: Identify major milestones in the business development process, such as product development, location acquisition, and market launch. Develop a timeline for achieving these milestones and monitor progress regularly.

7.2. Project Deadlines: Set deadlines for each phase of the business plan, including development, marketing, and operations. Ensure that deadlines are realistic and achievable, and allocate resources accordingly.

7.3. Responsibilities: Assign responsibilities for each aspect of the implementation process. Develop a project management plan to ensure that tasks are completed on time and within budget.

7.4. Monitoring and Evaluation: Establish metrics for monitoring progress and evaluating performance. Regularly review the implementation process and make adjustments as needed to stay on track and achieve business goals.

2.1 Key Elements of a Business Plan

A well-crafted business plan serves as the blueprint for launching and managing a successful automated pizza machine business. It outlines the strategic direction, operational framework, and financial projections necessary to achieve business objectives. The key elements of a business plan encompass several critical components that collectively provide a comprehensive view of the business. This section elaborates on each of these elements, detailing their importance and how they contribute to the overall success of the venture.

1. Executive Summary

1.1. Overview of the Business: The executive summary provides a snapshot of the entire business plan, summarizing the core concept, mission, and vision of the automated pizza machine business. It should clearly articulate the unique value proposition, the problem being solved, and the benefits to customers. This section is crucial as it sets the tone for the rest of the business plan and captures the interest of potential investors and stakeholders.

1.2. Business Objectives: This part outlines the primary goals of the business, including both short-term and long-term objectives. Short-term goals might include milestones like securing funding, launching the first set of machines, and achieving initial sales targets. Long-term objectives could involve scaling operations, expanding to new markets, and reaching profitability. Clear objectives help in guiding the business's strategy and measuring its progress.

1.3. Financial Summary: A brief financial overview is essential to provide insights into the financial viability of the business. This includes initial funding requirements, revenue projections, and expected profitability. Key financial metrics such as break-even analysis, cash flow forecasts, and financial ratios should be highlighted to demonstrate the potential return on investment and financial health of the business.

2. Market Analysis

2.1. Industry Overview: The market analysis section provides a detailed examination of the industry landscape, including trends, growth opportunities, and challenges. This includes understanding the current state of the vending machine market, technological advancements, and consumer preferences. An in-depth industry analysis helps in identifying potential market gaps and positioning the business effectively.

2.2. Competitive Analysis: This component involves evaluating the competitive environment by identifying key competitors, analyzing their strengths and weaknesses, and understanding their market positioning. A thorough competitive analysis helps in developing strategies to differentiate the automated pizza machines from existing offerings and capturing a share of the market.

2.3. Target Market Identification: Define the target market segments for the automated pizza machines. This includes demographic details, geographic locations, and psychographic profiles of potential customers. Understanding the target market's needs, preferences, and purchasing behavior is essential for tailoring the product and marketing strategies to effectively reach and engage with customers.

2.4. Market Trends and Opportunities: Identify and analyze current market trends and emerging opportunities. This could include shifts in consumer behavior, technological advancements, and changes in regulatory environments. Recognizing these trends and opportunities helps in adapting the business strategy to align with market demands and capitalize on growth potential.

3. Product and Service Offering

3.1. Product Description: Provide a detailed description of the automated pizza machines, including their design, features, and technology. Highlight the unique aspects of the product, such as cooking technology, ingredient management, and customization options. A comprehensive product description helps in conveying the value and functionality of the machines to potential customers and investors.

3.2. Value Proposition: Articulate the value proposition of the automated pizza machines, focusing on the benefits they offer to customers. This includes convenience, quality, speed, and personalization. The value proposition should clearly differentiate the product from competitors and address the specific needs and preferences of the target market.

3.3. Service and Support: Outline the service and support provided to customers, including installation, maintenance, and customer service. Detail the processes for handling repairs, troubleshooting, and ensuring machine uptime. Providing robust service and support is crucial for maintaining customer satisfaction and operational efficiency.

3.4. Research and Development: Discuss any ongoing or planned research and development (R&D) activities aimed at improving the product or expanding the product line. This could include innovations in technology, new features, or enhancements based on customer feedback. R&D efforts demonstrate a commitment to continuous improvement and staying ahead of industry trends.

4. Operational Plan

4.1. Production Process: Describe the production process for the automated pizza machines, including sourcing materials, manufacturing, and quality control. Outline the steps involved in producing the machines, from design and prototyping to assembly and testing. A well-defined production process ensures consistency and reliability in the final product.

4.2. Supply Chain Management: Detail the supply chain logistics, including sourcing ingredients, managing inventory, and distributing products. Effective supply chain management is crucial for ensuring timely delivery and maintaining product quality. Discuss partnerships with suppliers and logistics providers to streamline operations and reduce costs.

4.3. Location Strategy: Identify the criteria for selecting locations for deploying the automated pizza machines. Consider factors such as foot traffic, target customer demographics, and accessibility. Develop a strategy for securing and managing locations, including negotiating leases or partnerships with property owners.

4.4. Staffing Requirements: Define the staffing needs for the business, including roles and responsibilities. This may include technical support staff, sales representatives, and operations personnel. Outline the recruitment process, training programs, and management structure to ensure that the business is adequately staffed and efficiently managed.

4.5. Technology Infrastructure: Describe the technology infrastructure required to support the automated pizza machines, including software systems for machine operation, data collection, and remote monitoring. Ensure that the technology infrastructure is robust and capable of handling operational demands.

5. Marketing and Sales Strategy

5.1. Marketing Plan: Develop a comprehensive marketing plan to promote the automated pizza machines. This includes identifying marketing channels, such as digital marketing, social media, and local advertising, and crafting targeted campaigns to reach the desired audience. The marketing plan should outline strategies for building brand awareness and generating leads.

5.2. Sales Strategy: Outline the sales approach for acquiring and managing customer accounts. This may include direct sales efforts, partnerships with businesses, and online sales channels. Develop strategies for building relationships with customers, addressing their needs, and driving sales growth.

5.3. Branding and Positioning: Define the brand identity and positioning for the automated pizza machines. This includes developing a brand message that resonates with the target audience and emphasizes the unique selling points of the product. Consistent branding and positioning are essential for building a strong market presence and differentiating the business.

5.4. Customer Acquisition and Retention: Develop strategies for acquiring new customers and retaining existing ones. This may include implementing loyalty programs, offering promotions, and gathering customer feedback to improve the product and service. Effective customer acquisition and retention strategies contribute to long-term business success.

6. Financial Plan

6.1. Startup Costs: Detail the initial costs required to launch the business, including expenses for equipment, technology, marketing, and operational setup. Developing a clear budget for startup costs helps in managing financial resources and planning for funding needs.

6.2. Revenue Projections: Provide revenue projections based on market research, pricing strategy, and sales forecasts. Include estimates for sales volume, pricing, and revenue growth over time. Accurate revenue projections are essential for evaluating the business's financial potential and planning for future growth.

6.3. Profitability Analysis: Conduct a profitability analysis to determine the break-even point and assess the potential for profitability. Analyze profit margins, cost structures, and financial ratios to evaluate the business's financial health and sustainability.

6.4. Funding Requirements: Identify the funding requirements for the business, including startup capital and working capital. Develop a funding strategy that may include equity investment, loans, or other financing options. Outline the use of funds and the expected return on investment for potential investors.

6.5. Financial Risks and Mitigation: Assess potential financial risks and develop strategies to mitigate them. This may include risks related to market fluctuations, operational challenges, and financial management. Developing contingency plans helps in managing uncertainties and ensuring business stability.

7. Implementation Timeline

7.1. Key Milestones: Identify major milestones in the business development process, such as product development, location acquisition, and market launch. Establish a timeline for achieving these milestones and monitor progress regularly to ensure that the business stays on track.

7.2. Project Deadlines: Set deadlines for each phase of the business plan, including development, marketing, and operations. Ensure that deadlines are realistic and achievable, and allocate resources accordingly to meet these deadlines.

7.3. Responsibilities: Assign responsibilities for each aspect of the implementation process. Develop a project management plan to ensure that tasks are completed on time and within budget. Clearly define roles and responsibilities to facilitate effective coordination and execution.

7.4. Monitoring and Evaluation: Establish metrics for monitoring progress and evaluating performance. Regularly review the implementation process and make adjustments as needed to stay on track and achieve business goals. Monitoring and evaluation help in identifying areas for improvement and ensuring the successful execution of the business plan.

2.2 Defining Your Value Proposition

A compelling value proposition is fundamental to the success of any business, particularly in a niche market such as automated pizza machines. It succinctly articulates why customers should choose your product over competitors, highlighting the unique benefits and value that your business offers. Crafting a clear and persuasive value proposition involves understanding customer needs, differentiating from competitors, and effectively communicating the benefits of your offering. This section provides a comprehensive guide to defining a robust value proposition for an automated pizza machine business.

1. Understanding Customer Needs

1.1. Identifying Pain Points: To create a compelling value proposition, begin by identifying the pain points and needs of your target customers. For automated pizza machines, this might include issues such as the need for quick and convenient food options, consistent quality, or a desire for customization. Conduct market research, surveys, and customer interviews to gain insights into what customers are looking for in a food service solution.

1.2. Analyzing Customer Preferences: Understand the preferences of your target market regarding pizza, such as favorite toppings, dietary restrictions, and preferred portion sizes. This information helps in designing a product that aligns with customer tastes and expectations. Analyze trends in consumer behavior, such as the increasing demand for on-demand food services and technological convenience, to tailor your offering accordingly.

1.3. Assessing Customer Value: Determine what aspects of your automated pizza machine will deliver the most value to customers. This could be convenience, quality, speed, or the novelty of using an automated system. Understanding what customers value most allows you to focus on these elements in your value proposition.

2. Differentiating from Competitors

2.1. Identifying Unique Selling Points: To differentiate your automated pizza machine from competitors, identify and emphasize its unique selling points (USPs). These could include advanced cooking technology, the ability to customize pizzas to individual preferences, or a distinctive design. Highlight what makes your product stand out and why it provides superior value compared to existing solutions.

2.2. Evaluating Competitor Offerings: Analyze the strengths and weaknesses of competitors in the automated pizza machine market. Assess their product features, pricing, customer service, and market positioning. Use this analysis to identify gaps in the market and opportunities for differentiation. Understanding the competitive landscape helps in positioning your value proposition effectively.

2.3. Leveraging Technology and Innovation: Showcase any technological innovations or advancements that set your automated pizza machine apart. This could include proprietary cooking methods, integrated payment systems, or user-friendly interfaces. Emphasizing technological advantages can help in attracting tech-savvy customers and positioning your product as a leader in innovation.

3. Crafting the Value Proposition

3.1. Articulating Key Benefits: Clearly articulate the key benefits of your automated pizza machine. Focus on how the product solves customer problems or meets their needs more effectively than alternatives. For instance, emphasize how the machine provides high-quality pizza quickly and conveniently, or how it allows for extensive customization to suit individual preferences.

3.2. Communicating Differentiation: Convey how your automated pizza machine is different from and superior to competitor products. Use clear, concise language to highlight the unique features and advantages of your offering. Ensure that your messaging resonates with your target audience and clearly demonstrates the value they will receive.

3.3. Providing Evidence and Support: Support your value proposition with evidence such as customer testimonials, case studies, or performance metrics. Demonstrating real-world success and customer satisfaction can enhance credibility and reinforce the value proposition. Providing evidence helps build trust with potential customers and stakeholders.

3.4. Refining the Message: Continuously refine your value proposition based on feedback and market conditions. Test different messaging approaches to determine what resonates best with your target audience. Adapt your value proposition as needed to stay relevant and aligned with customer expectations and market trends.

4. Integrating the Value Proposition into Business Strategy

4.1. Aligning Marketing Efforts: Ensure that your value proposition is integrated into all marketing and promotional activities. This includes your website, advertising campaigns, social media, and sales materials. Consistent messaging reinforces the value proposition and helps in building a strong brand identity.

4.2. Training Sales and Support Teams: Equip your sales and support teams with a thorough understanding of the value proposition. Train them to communicate the benefits effectively and address customer inquiries or objections. A well-informed team is crucial for delivering a compelling sales pitch and providing excellent customer service.

4.3. Monitoring and Adjusting: Regularly monitor the effectiveness of your value proposition and make adjustments as needed. Gather feedback from customers, analyze market trends, and review competitive developments to ensure that your value proposition remains relevant and compelling. Continuous improvement helps in maintaining a competitive edge and meeting evolving customer needs.

2.3 SWOT Analysis (Strengths, Weaknesses, Opportunities, and Threats)

A SWOT analysis is a strategic planning tool used to identify and evaluate the Strengths, Weaknesses, Opportunities, and Threats related to a business or project. For an automated pizza machine business, conducting a SWOT analysis provides valuable insights into internal and external factors that can impact success. This analysis helps in developing strategies to leverage strengths, address weaknesses, seize opportunities, and mitigate threats. Here's a comprehensive breakdown of each component of the SWOT analysis for an automated pizza machine venture:

1. Strengths

1.1. Innovative Technology: One of the key strengths of an automated pizza machine business is the use of cutting-edge technology. Advanced cooking mechanisms, automated ingredient dispensing, and user-friendly interfaces can set the product apart from traditional food service solutions. Emphasizing these technological advancements can attract tech-savvy customers and position the product as a leader in innovation.

1.2. Convenience and Speed: Automated pizza machines offer significant convenience and speed compared to conventional pizza outlets. Customers can get freshly made pizza quickly, reducing wait times and providing an efficient solution for those on the go. This convenience is a strong selling point and can drive customer preference.

1.3. Consistency and Quality: The automation of the pizza-making process ensures consistent quality and taste with every order. Automated machines can standardize ingredient amounts, cooking times, and temperatures, leading to uniform product quality. This consistency can enhance customer satisfaction and loyalty.

1.4. 24/7 Operation: Unlike traditional pizza restaurants, automated machines can operate around the clock without the need for staff. This capability allows the business to serve customers at any time, increasing potential sales and catering to varying schedules and preferences.

1.5. Low Labor Costs: Automated pizza machines reduce the need for extensive staffing, which can lower labor costs. The reduction in labor requirements can also simplify operations and decrease the complexities associated with managing a workforce.

2. Weaknesses

2.1. High Initial Investment: The development and deployment of automated pizza machines often require a significant initial investment. Costs include research and development, production, and installation. This high upfront expenditure can be a barrier to entry and may require substantial funding or financing.

2.2. Maintenance and Technical Issues: Automated systems are prone to technical malfunctions and require regular maintenance. Ensuring that machines are operational and addressing technical issues promptly can be challenging. Maintenance costs and potential downtime can impact overall profitability and customer satisfaction.

2.3. Limited Human Interaction: The automated nature of the pizza machine reduces direct human interaction, which might affect customer experience for those who value personal service. In scenarios where customer service is crucial, the lack of human touch could be a disadvantage.

2.4. Product Limitations: While automated machines can offer a range of pizza options, they may have limitations in terms of customization and menu variety compared to traditional pizzerias. This could restrict the appeal of the product to certain customer segments.

2.5. Dependence on Technology: The business heavily relies on technology, which can be a double-edged sword. Any technological glitches, software bugs, or system failures can disrupt operations and negatively impact customer experience.

3. Opportunities

3.1. Growing Demand for Convenience: There is a rising consumer demand for convenient food solutions. Automated pizza machines cater to this trend by providing a quick and easy way to obtain freshly made pizza. Capitalizing on this demand can drive growth and expansion opportunities.

3.2. Expansion into New Markets: The automated pizza machine business has the potential to expand into various markets, including high-traffic locations such as airports, shopping malls, universities, and office buildings. Exploring new geographical regions and diverse market segments can lead to increased revenue streams.

3.3. Technological Advancements: Ongoing advancements in technology present opportunities for innovation and improvement. Incorporating emerging technologies such as artificial intelligence, IoT (Internet of Things), and machine learning can enhance machine capabilities, optimize performance, and offer advanced features.

3.4. Partnerships and Collaborations: Collaborating with other businesses, such as real estate developers, convenience stores, or food service companies, can create strategic partnerships that enhance market reach and operational efficiency. These partnerships can provide access to prime locations and additional resources.

3.5. Health and Dietary Trends: As consumer preferences shift towards healthier eating habits, there is an opportunity to cater to these trends by offering a range of healthier pizza options, including whole grain crusts, organic ingredients, and customizable toppings. Adapting to dietary trends can attract a broader customer base.

4. Threats

4.1. Intense Competition: The food service industry is highly competitive, with numerous players ranging from traditional pizzerias to other automated food solutions. Competing with established brands and new entrants can be challenging, requiring continuous innovation and differentiation.

4.2. Economic Fluctuations: Economic downturns or fluctuations can impact consumer spending on non-essential items, including convenience foods. Economic instability may lead to reduced customer spending and affect sales performance.

4.3. Regulatory and Compliance Issues: Compliance with health and safety regulations, food handling standards, and local ordinances is essential for operating automated pizza machines. Regulatory changes or strict compliance requirements can increase operational costs and affect business operations.

4.4. Technological Disruptions: Rapid technological advancements can lead to the development of new and improved automated food solutions. Staying ahead of technological disruptions and maintaining a competitive edge requires continuous investment in research and development.

4.5. Customer Acceptance: Consumer acceptance of automated food machines may vary based on cultural preferences, attitudes towards automation, and perceived value. Overcoming resistance to change and convincing customers of the benefits of automated pizza machines is crucial for market adoption.

2.4 Financial Planning and Profit Projections

Financial planning and profit projections are critical components of a business plan, providing a roadmap for managing resources, forecasting profitability, and ensuring the financial health of the automated pizza machine business. This section covers the essential aspects of financial planning, including setting budgets, projecting revenues and expenses, and evaluating profitability. A thorough financial plan helps in making informed decisions, securing funding, and guiding the business toward achieving its financial goals.

1. Budgeting and Financial Planning

1.1. Initial Startup Costs: Estimate the initial investment required to launch the automated pizza machine business. This includes costs for product development, manufacturing, purchasing machines, securing locations, marketing, and legal fees. Accurately forecasting these costs is crucial for securing financing and managing cash flow. Key components of startup costs may include:

- Research and Development: Costs associated with designing and prototyping the automated pizza machines.

- Equipment and Machinery: Expenses for purchasing or leasing the machines and related technology.

- Location Setup: Costs for securing and preparing locations, including lease agreements and site improvements.

- Marketing and Branding: Budget for initial marketing campaigns, promotional materials, and branding efforts.

- Legal and Administrative Fees: Fees for business registration, permits, licenses, and legal consultations.

1.2. Operational Expenses: Outline the ongoing operational expenses necessary for running the business. These include:

- Maintenance Costs: Regular maintenance and repair costs for the automated pizza machines.

- Ingredient Costs: Costs for purchasing pizza ingredients, including dough, sauce, cheese, and toppings.

- Utilities: Expenses for electricity, water, and other utilities required to operate the machines.

- Staffing Costs: If applicable, salaries for any support staff involved in operations, maintenance, or customer service.

- Insurance: Costs for insuring the machines, locations, and business operations.

1.3. Cash Flow Management: Develop a cash flow management plan to ensure that the business has sufficient liquidity to cover expenses and manage day-to-day operations. This involves:

- Cash Flow Forecasting: Projecting monthly cash inflows and outflows to identify potential cash shortfalls or surpluses.

- Managing Receivables and Payables: Establishing processes for invoicing, collecting payments, and managing accounts payable to maintain healthy cash flow.

2. Revenue Projections

2.1. Sales Forecasting: Estimate the expected sales volume and revenue from the automated pizza machines. Consider factors such as:

- Machine Placement: Anticipate sales based on the number of machines deployed and their locations.

- Pricing Strategy: Set pricing for pizzas, factoring in ingredient costs, operational expenses, and desired profit margins.

- Market Demand: Analyze market demand and customer preferences to project realistic sales figures.

2.2. Revenue Streams:

Identify potential revenue streams beyond the direct sale of pizzas. These may include:

- Advertising Partnerships: Revenue from advertising or branding partnerships with local businesses.

- Franchise Opportunities: Income from franchising the automated pizza machine concept to other operators.

- Subscription Models: Offering subscription services or loyalty programs for frequent customers.

2.3. Seasonality and Trends: Consider the impact of seasonality and market trends on revenue projections. For example:

- Seasonal Variations: Account for potential fluctuations in sales due to seasonal factors, such as holidays or weather conditions.

- Emerging Trends: Incorporate trends such as increased demand for convenience foods or technological advancements that could affect sales.

3. Profitability Analysis

3.1. Break-Even Analysis: Conduct a break-even analysis to determine the point at which total revenue equals total costs, and the business starts generating a profit. This involves:

- Fixed Costs: Identifying fixed costs that do not change with the level of production or sales, such as lease payments and salaries.

- Variable Costs: Calculating variable costs that fluctuate with production levels, such as ingredient costs and maintenance.

- Break-Even Point Calculation: Using the formula to calculate the break-even point in units or revenue.

3.2. Profit Margins: Calculate profit margins to assess the profitability of the business. Key profit margins include:

- Gross Profit Margin: The difference between revenue and the cost of goods sold, expressed as a percentage of revenue.

- Net Profit Margin: The difference between total revenue and total expenses, expressed as a percentage of revenue.

3.3. Financial Ratios: Analyze key financial ratios to evaluate the financial health of the business. Important ratios include:

- Return on Investment (ROI): Measures the return generated on invested capital.

- Current Ratio: Assesses the business's ability to meet short-term obligations with current assets.

- Debt-to-Equity Ratio: Evaluates the business's leverage and financial stability.

4. Funding Requirements and Strategies

4.1. Capital Needs: Determine the total capital required to start and sustain the business. This includes initial startup costs and working capital for ongoing operations.

4.2. Funding Sources: Explore various funding options to meet capital needs. Potential sources of funding include:

- Equity Investment: Raising funds by selling shares in the business to investors.

- Loans: Securing loans from financial institutions or lenders.

- Grants and Subsidies: Applying for grants or subsidies from government programs or industry organizations.

- Crowdfunding: Utilizing crowdfunding platforms to raise capital from a large number of individuals.

4.3. Financial Projections: Prepare detailed financial projections to present to potential investors or lenders. This includes:

- Profit and Loss Statements: Projected income statements showing expected revenue, expenses, and profit over a specified period.

- Balance Sheets: Projected balance sheets detailing assets, liabilities, and equity.

- Cash Flow Statements: Projected cash flow statements showing expected cash inflows and outflows.

5. Risk Management

5.1. Identifying Financial Risks: Assess potential financial risks that could impact the business, such as economic downturns, fluctuating ingredient costs, or unexpected maintenance expenses.

5.2. Mitigation Strategies: Develop strategies to mitigate financial risks, including:

- Contingency Planning: Setting aside reserve funds to cover unexpected expenses.

- Insurance Coverage: Obtaining insurance to protect against financial losses due to unforeseen events.

Chapter 3:
Technological and Operational Aspects

In the realm of automated pizza machines, technological and operational aspects are crucial to ensuring that the business runs efficiently, meets customer expectations, and maintains a competitive edge. This chapter delves into the key technological components, operational procedures, and best practices necessary for the successful deployment and management of automated pizza machines.

1. Technological Components

1.1. Machine Design and Engineering

1.1.1. Mechanical Engineering: Automated pizza machines require sophisticated mechanical engineering to handle the various stages of pizza preparation. This includes dough kneading, sauce spreading, cheese application, and baking. The mechanical components must be durable, precise, and capable of operating continuously.

1.1.2. Cooking Technology: The choice of cooking technology significantly impacts the quality of the pizza. Options include convection ovens, conveyor ovens, or combination ovens that can handle high temperatures and ensure even cooking. The technology should be optimized for speed and consistency to meet customer demands.

1.1.3. Dispensing Systems: Efficient ingredient dispensing systems are vital for consistency and quality. These systems must accurately measure and dispense ingredients such as dough, sauce, cheese, and toppings. Automated dispensers should be designed to minimize waste and prevent contamination.

1.2. Software and Control Systems

1.2.1. User Interface: The user interface (UI) is a critical component of the automated pizza machine. It should be intuitive and user-friendly, allowing customers to easily customize their pizza orders. The UI may include a touchscreen, voice commands, or mobile app integration.

1.2.2. Operational Software: The operational software controls the various functions of the pizza machine, including cooking times, ingredient dispensing, and machine diagnostics. It should be designed for reliability and ease of updates to accommodate new features or improvements.

1.2.3. Remote Monitoring: Remote monitoring capabilities allow operators to track machine performance, manage inventory, and perform diagnostics from a distance. This technology can help in identifying and resolving issues quickly, reducing downtime, and ensuring consistent operation.

1.3. Payment and Security Systems

1.3.1. Payment Processing: Automated pizza machines should support various payment methods, including credit/debit cards, mobile payments, and contactless transactions. Integration with payment processors should be secure and reliable to ensure smooth transactions.

1.3.2. Security Features: Security features are essential to protect the machine from theft and vandalism. This may include surveillance cameras, alarm systems, and secure access controls. Ensuring the security of the machine also involves protecting customer data and payment information.

2. Operational Procedures

2.1. Machine Installation and Setup

2.1.1. Site Selection: Choosing the right location for the automated pizza machine is crucial. High-traffic areas such as shopping malls, universities, or transportation hubs are ideal. The site should have adequate space, access to utilities, and proper visibility.

2.1.2. Installation Process: The installation process involves setting up the machine, connecting it to power and water sources, and calibrating the system for optimal performance. Professional installation may be required to ensure that all components are correctly assembled and functional.

2.1.3. Initial Testing: After installation, conduct thorough testing to ensure that the machine operates correctly. This includes testing the cooking cycle, ingredient dispensing, payment processing, and user interface. Address any issues identified during testing before the machine goes live.

2.2. Inventory Management

2.2.1. Ingredient Supply: Managing inventory of pizza ingredients is crucial for maintaining consistent product quality and avoiding shortages. Implement inventory management systems to track ingredient levels, order supplies, and monitor expiration dates.

2.2.2. Storage Conditions: Proper storage conditions are essential to maintain ingredient freshness and safety. Ensure that ingredients are stored in appropriate temperatures and conditions to prevent spoilage and contamination.

2.2.3. Supplier Relations: Establish strong relationships with reliable suppliers to ensure timely delivery of high-quality ingredients. Negotiate favorable terms and maintain clear communication to manage inventory effectively.

2.3. Maintenance and Support

2.3.1. Routine Maintenance: Regular maintenance is necessary to keep the automated pizza machine in optimal working condition. This includes cleaning, checking for wear and tear, and replacing parts as needed. Establish a maintenance schedule and adhere to it to prevent breakdowns and extend the machine's lifespan.

2.3.2. Technical Support: Provide access to technical support for troubleshooting and resolving any issues that may arise. This could involve on-site support, remote assistance, or a dedicated helpdesk. Quick and effective support is crucial for minimizing downtime and ensuring customer satisfaction.

2.3.3. Software Updates: Regular software updates are necessary to enhance functionality, address security vulnerabilities, and improve performance. Implement a system for managing and deploying updates to keep the operational software current and effective.

3. Quality Control

3.1. Consistency Checks: Implement procedures for checking the consistency of the pizza produced by the machine. This includes ensuring that cooking times, ingredient portions, and product appearance meet established standards.

3.2. Customer Feedback: Collect and analyze customer feedback to identify areas for improvement. Use feedback to make adjustments to the machine's settings, recipe formulations, or user interface to enhance the overall customer experience.

3.3. Compliance with Standards: Ensure that the automated pizza machine complies with relevant health, safety, and food quality standards. This includes adherence to local regulations and industry best practices for food safety and equipment operation.

4. Scalability and Growth

4.1. Scaling Operations: Plan for scaling the business by evaluating the feasibility of deploying additional machines in new locations. Consider factors such as market demand, logistical support, and financial resources when planning for expansion.

4.2. Technology Upgrades: Stay abreast of technological advancements that can enhance the performance and capabilities of automated pizza machines. Invest in upgrades that improve efficiency, functionality, or customer experience.

4.3. Expansion Strategies: Develop strategies for expanding the business, including identifying new market opportunities, forming partnerships, and exploring franchise models. A well-thought-out expansion plan can drive growth and increase market presence.

3.1 Types of Pizza Vending Machines

1. Traditional Pizza Vending Machines

- Description: Traditional pizza vending machines typically store pre-cooked or frozen pizzas, which are heated and served to the customer upon request. These machines are often found in high-traffic areas such as train stations, airports, and university campuses.

Features:
- Pre-cooked Pizza Storage: The machine houses a selection of pre-cooked or frozen pizzas that can be quickly reheated.
- Simple Operation: Customers select their desired pizza from a menu, and the machine automatically heats it up and dispenses it.

Pros:

- Ease of Implementation: These machines are straightforward to set up and operate, requiring minimal technical complexity.
- Lower Initial Costs: Compared to more advanced models, traditional vending machines have relatively low upfront costs.
- Minimal Maintenance: With fewer moving parts and simpler technology, these machines generally require less maintenance.

Cons:

- Limited Freshness: Since pizzas are pre-cooked or frozen, the freshness and quality might not be as high as that of freshly made pizzas.

- Limited Customization: These machines offer minimal or no customization options for the consumer.

2. Fully Automated Pizza Ovens

- Description: Fully automated pizza ovens are advanced machines that handle the entire pizza-making process, including dough preparation, topping assembly, and baking. These systems use automation to ensure consistent quality and freshness.

Features:

- Real-Time Cooking: Ingredients are processed and baked on demand, offering fresh pizza to customers.
- Advanced Technology: These machines often incorporate sophisticated technology to manage dough kneading, sauce application, and topping distribution.

Pros:

- High Quality and Freshness: Because pizzas are made fresh on-site, the quality and taste are generally superior.
- Customization: Many models allow customers to customize their pizzas by selecting ingredients and toppings through a user-friendly interface.
- Interactive Experience: The process is often engaging for customers, providing a unique and modern dining experience.

Cons:

- Higher Costs: The initial investment for these machines can be substantial due to the advanced technology and components involved.
- Regular Maintenance: These machines require ongoing maintenance and technical support to ensure smooth operation.
- Ingredient Management: Requires efficient supply chain management to keep fresh ingredients in stock.

3. Pizza Vending Machines with Customization Options

- Description: These machines provide customers with the ability to customize their pizzas by choosing from a variety of ingredients and toppings. They often feature interactive touch screens or mobile apps for placing orders.

Features:

- Customizable Orders: Customers can create their own pizza combinations based on a wide selection of ingredients.

- User Interface: Typically equipped with digital interfaces that make it easy to select and pay for customized orders.

Pros:

- Enhanced Customer Satisfaction: Customization allows customers to tailor their pizzas to their preferences, increasing satisfaction.
- Attracts a Broader Audience: By offering a variety of choices, these machines appeal to a diverse customer base.

Cons:

- Technological Complexity: These machines are more complex, requiring advanced software and hardware to manage custom orders.
- Inventory Management: Requires precise management of a wider range of ingredients to ensure availability and freshness.

4. Hybrid Pizza Vending Machines

- Description: Hybrid machines combine elements of traditional vending machines with features of fully automated pizza ovens. They offer a mix of pre-cooked pizzas and options for fresh preparation.

Features:

- Versatility: Provides both pre-cooked and freshly made pizza options, offering flexibility in product offerings.
- Balance of Technology: Incorporates aspects of automation while retaining some of the simplicity of traditional models.

Pros:

- Flexibility: Can cater to different customer preferences by offering both pre-cooked and freshly prepared options.
- Cost-Effective: Balances cost and technological investment, potentially offering a good compromise between traditional and fully automated models.

Cons:

- Complex Operations: Managing both types of offerings may complicate operations and inventory management.
- Potential Compromises: Might not achieve the same level of freshness or customization as specialized machines.

5. Premium Pizza Vending Machines

- Description: Premium vending machines are designed to offer high-end, gourmet pizzas using high-quality ingredients and advanced cooking technology. These machines are often found in upscale locations or specialty food venues.

Features:

- High-Quality Ingredients: Uses premium ingredients to deliver a gourmet pizza experience.
- Advanced Technology: Incorporates state-of-the-art systems for quality control and cooking precision.

Pros:

- Superior Quality: Offers a high-end pizza experience, attracting customers willing to pay a premium.
- Attractive to Niche Markets: Appeals to a specific market segment looking for gourmet food options.

Cons:

- Significant Investment: Requires a large initial investment due to the high cost of equipment and ingredients.
- Target Market: May not be suitable for all locations or customer demographics, limiting potential market reach.

6. Mobile Pizza Vending Units

- Description: Mobile pizza vending units are designed to be moved to different locations, such as events, fairs, or temporary pop-up spots. These units offer a flexible solution for reaching various markets.

Features:

- Portability: Can be relocated to different locations based on demand or special events.
- Adaptability: Provides a convenient way to test new markets or reach customers in different areas.

Pros:

- Flexible Location: Can adapt to changing customer needs and seasonal demands by moving to high-traffic areas.
- Event Opportunities: Ideal for temporary or special events, enhancing visibility and sales opportunities.

Cons:

- Logistical Challenges: Requires careful planning for transportation, setup, and maintenance.
- Space Constraints: Limited space may restrict the range of products and amenities offered.

3.2 Cutting-Edge Technologies: From Automated Cooking to Customization

1. Automated Cooking Systems

- Description: Automated cooking systems represent the pinnacle of technology in pizza vending machines, enabling precise control over the entire pizza-making process, from dough preparation to baking.

Components:

- Dough Handling Units: These machines automatically mix, knead, and portion dough to ensure consistency and quality in every pizza. Advanced models include automated dough stretching and shaping mechanisms.
- Topping Dispensers: Automated dispensers accurately apply sauces, cheeses, and other toppings. These systems are calibrated to ensure the correct amount of each ingredient, reducing waste and maintaining consistency.
- Baking Chambers: Equipped with high-efficiency ovens, these systems use advanced heating elements and precise temperature controls to bake pizzas evenly and quickly. Some models feature conveyor belts or rotating trays to enhance baking uniformity.

Pros:

- Consistency: Provides uniform quality and taste in every pizza, reducing human error and variability.
- Efficiency: Accelerates the pizza-making process, offering faster service and high throughput.

Cons:

- High Initial Costs: These systems are often expensive to install due to the advanced technology and components involved.
- Maintenance Needs: Requires regular maintenance and technical support to ensure optimal performance.

2. Advanced Customization Features

- Description: Advanced customization features allow customers to personalize their pizzas by choosing ingredients, toppings, and cooking preferences through intuitive interfaces.

Components:

- Touchscreen Interfaces: Many machines are equipped with large touchscreens that enable users to easily select and customize their pizza options. These interfaces often provide visual representations of the pizza as it is being customized.
- Mobile Integration: Some vending machines offer integration with mobile apps, allowing customers to place and customize orders remotely. This feature can include real-time order tracking and payment processing.
- AI-Powered Recommendations: Artificial intelligence algorithms analyze customer preferences and past orders to offer personalized recommendations and optimize ingredient combinations.

Pros:

- Enhanced User Experience: Provides a tailored experience, making the ordering process more engaging and satisfying for customers.
- Increased Sales: Personalized options can drive higher sales by catering to individual preferences and dietary needs.

Cons:

- Complexity: Requires sophisticated software and hardware integration, increasing the complexity of the machine.
- Data Management: Involves managing large amounts of customer data and preferences, which requires robust data security measures.

3. Ingredient Management and Dispensing Technology

- Description: Modern pizza vending machines utilize advanced ingredient management and dispensing technologies to ensure ingredient freshness and accuracy.

Components:

- Climate-Controlled Storage: Ingredients are stored in climate-controlled compartments to maintain optimal freshness and prevent spoilage. This feature is crucial for perishable items such as cheeses and vegetables.
- Precision Dispensing: Advanced dispensing systems measure and release precise amounts of ingredients to avoid waste and ensure consistent quality.

- Real-Time Inventory Tracking: Sensors and software track ingredient levels in real-time, alerting operators when supplies are running low and enabling timely restocking.

Pros:

- Freshness: Helps maintain ingredient quality and prolong shelf life, contributing to a better overall product.
- Efficiency: Reduces waste and ensures that ingredients are used efficiently.

Cons:

- Higher Costs: Advanced storage and dispensing systems can increase the initial investment and operational costs.
- Maintenance: Requires regular checks and maintenance to ensure that dispensing mechanisms and storage units are functioning correctly.

4. Self-Cleaning and Hygiene Technologies

- Description: To ensure food safety and maintain high hygiene standards, modern pizza vending machines incorporate self-cleaning technologies and hygiene monitoring systems.

Components:

- Automatic Cleaning Cycles: Some machines feature automated cleaning cycles that sanitize cooking surfaces, dispensers, and other components. These cycles use high-pressure water, steam, or cleaning agents to maintain cleanliness.
- UV Sterilization: Ultraviolet (UV) light is used to sterilize surfaces and kill harmful bacteria, ensuring a hygienic environment for food preparation.
- Hygiene Sensors: Sensors monitor the cleanliness of various components and alert operators to potential issues, ensuring compliance with health and safety regulations.

Pros:

- Food Safety: Enhances food safety by maintaining high standards of cleanliness and reducing the risk of contamination.
- Convenience: Reduces the need for manual cleaning, saving time and labor costs.

Cons:

- Cost: Self-cleaning and hygiene technologies can add to the overall cost of the machine.

- Technical Complexity: These systems add complexity to the machine, which may require specialized maintenance.

5. Data Analytics and Remote Monitoring

- Description: Advanced pizza vending machines incorporate data analytics and remote monitoring capabilities to optimize performance and operational efficiency.

Components:

- Remote Monitoring Systems: Operators can monitor the machine's performance, ingredient levels, and maintenance needs remotely through cloud-based platforms or mobile apps.
- Data Analytics: Analytics tools analyze sales data, customer preferences, and machine performance to identify trends, optimize operations, and make data-driven decisions.
- Predictive Maintenance: Machine learning algorithms predict when maintenance is needed based on usage patterns and performance data, helping to prevent unexpected breakdowns.

Pros:

- Operational Efficiency: Enhances operational efficiency by providing insights into machine performance and customer behavior.
- Proactive Maintenance: Reduces downtime by identifying and addressing maintenance issues before they cause problems.

Cons:

- Data Security: Handling and storing large amounts of data require robust security measures to protect sensitive information.
- Complexity: Implementing and managing data analytics and remote monitoring systems adds to the complexity of the vending machine.

6. Sustainable Technologies

- Description: As sustainability becomes increasingly important, modern pizza vending machines are incorporating technologies aimed at reducing environmental impact.

Components:

- Energy-Efficient Systems: Advanced ovens and cooling systems use energy-efficient technologies to reduce power consumption and lower operating costs.

- Recycling and Waste Management: Machines may include features for recycling packaging materials and managing food waste, contributing to a more sustainable operation.
- Eco-Friendly Materials: Use of biodegradable or recyclable materials in the construction of the machine and its packaging helps reduce environmental impact.

Pros:

- Environmental Impact: Reduces the carbon footprint and supports sustainable practices, which can be attractive to environmentally conscious consumers.
- Cost Savings: Energy-efficient technologies can lower utility costs over time.

Cons:

- Initial Investment: Sustainable technologies may require a higher initial investment, which could be a barrier for some operators.
- Implementation Challenges: Integrating and managing eco-friendly practices can be complex and require additional planning.

3.3 Managing Day-to-Day Operations

1. Operational Workflow

- Description: Managing day-to-day operations in a pizza vending machine business involves overseeing the entire workflow from machine maintenance to customer service. It ensures that the machines function smoothly and efficiently, providing a consistent customer experience.

Key Components:

- Routine Checks: Daily checks of the vending machines to ensure they are operational. This includes verifying that all components, such as the heating elements, dispensers, and interfaces, are functioning correctly.
- Ingredient Restocking: Regular restocking of ingredients and supplies to ensure that the machines are always ready to serve customers. This involves tracking inventory levels and scheduling deliveries.
- Cleaning and Maintenance: Implementing a cleaning schedule to keep the machines hygienic and operational. This includes both manual cleaning and automated self-cleaning cycles if available.
- Customer Support: Providing support to customers in case of issues such as machine malfunctions or order problems. This can involve on-site support or remote troubleshooting.

Pros:

- Efficiency: Regular monitoring and maintenance prevent unexpected breakdowns and ensure continuous operation.
- Customer Satisfaction: Proper management leads to fewer service disruptions, enhancing customer experience and satisfaction.

Cons:

- Resource Intensive: Requires dedicated personnel or systems to manage daily tasks effectively, which can be resource-intensive.
- Potential Downtime: Despite best efforts, occasional downtime may occur, which can impact service and customer satisfaction.

2. Inventory Management

- Description: Effective inventory management is crucial for ensuring that the vending machines are stocked with fresh ingredients and operational supplies. It involves tracking inventory levels, managing suppliers, and optimizing stock levels.

Key Components:

- Inventory Tracking: Use of inventory management software or systems to monitor stock levels in real-time. This helps in predicting when ingredients need to be replenished and avoids overstocking.
- Supplier Coordination: Maintaining relationships with suppliers to ensure timely delivery of ingredients and supplies. This involves negotiating contracts and managing supplier performance.
- Stock Rotation: Implementing a system for rotating stock to ensure that ingredients are used within their shelf life and to minimize waste.

Pros:

- Cost Control: Effective inventory management helps in controlling costs by reducing waste and preventing stockouts.
- Operational Efficiency: Ensures that machines are always stocked with necessary ingredients, reducing service interruptions.

Cons:

- Complexity: Managing inventory involves coordinating with multiple suppliers and maintaining accurate records, which can be complex.
- Storage Requirements: Requires adequate storage facilities for ingredients, which may add to operational costs.

3. Machine Maintenance and Troubleshooting

- Description: Regular maintenance and prompt troubleshooting are essential for keeping pizza vending machines in optimal working condition. This includes both preventive and corrective maintenance practices.

Key Components:

- Preventive Maintenance: Scheduled maintenance tasks designed to prevent issues before they arise. This includes checking and servicing mechanical parts, updating software, and inspecting key components.
- Corrective Maintenance: Addressing issues as they occur, such as repairing or replacing malfunctioning parts. This may involve on-site repairs or technical support.
- Troubleshooting: Identifying and resolving issues reported by customers or detected through monitoring systems. This involves diagnosing problems and implementing fixes promptly.

Pros:

- Minimized Downtime: Regular maintenance reduces the likelihood of machine breakdowns, ensuring consistent service.
- Longer Equipment Life: Proper care extends the lifespan of the machines, providing better long-term value.

Cons:

- Costs: Maintenance and troubleshooting can incur costs, including labor, parts, and service fees.
- Complexity: Requires technical expertise to address various issues and maintain sophisticated equipment.

4. Financial Management

- Description: Effective financial management is crucial for maintaining profitability and ensuring the financial health of the pizza vending machine business. This includes budgeting, accounting, and financial reporting.

Key Components:

- Budgeting: Developing and managing a budget that covers operational costs, including maintenance, inventory, and staffing. Regularly reviewing and adjusting the budget to align with actual expenses and revenue.
- Accounting: Keeping accurate financial records of all transactions, including sales, expenses, and payments. This involves managing accounts payable and receivable.

- Financial Reporting: Generating regular financial reports to monitor performance, analyze profitability, and make informed business decisions.

Pros:

- Financial Control: Provides oversight of financial performance and helps in identifying areas for cost savings and revenue enhancement.
- Decision Making: Accurate financial data supports strategic decision-making and helps in setting financial goals.

Cons:

- Complexity: Financial management involves various tasks and requires attention to detail, which can be time-consuming.
- Requires Expertise: May require specialized knowledge or hiring of financial professionals to manage effectively.

5. Compliance and Safety

- Description: Ensuring compliance with health, safety, and regulatory standards is essential for operating pizza vending machines legally and safely. This involves adhering to food safety regulations and maintaining safe operating conditions.

Key Components:

- Health and Safety Regulations: Compliance with local and national food safety standards, including proper handling and storage of ingredients, and maintaining hygienic conditions.
- Regulatory Compliance: Adhering to regulations related to vending machine operations, such as licensing, permits, and inspections.
- Safety Procedures: Implementing safety procedures for both machine operation and customer interactions, including emergency protocols and training for staff.

Pros:

- Legal Compliance: Reduces the risk of legal issues and fines by ensuring adherence to regulations and standards.
- Customer Trust: Builds trust with customers by providing safe and hygienic products.

Cons:

- Regulatory Burden: Compliance can involve complex regulations and frequent inspections, which can be challenging to manage.

- Costs: Meeting safety and compliance requirements may involve additional costs, such as for certifications and inspections.

6. Customer Engagement and Feedback

- Description: Engaging with customers and gathering feedback is crucial for improving the vending machine experience and addressing any issues. This involves collecting and analyzing customer opinions and responding to their needs.

Key Components:

- Feedback Channels: Providing channels for customers to give feedback, such as surveys, comment cards, or digital interfaces on the vending machines.
- Customer Interaction: Engaging with customers through social media or direct communication to build relationships and address concerns.
- Service Improvements: Using customer feedback to identify areas for improvement and make necessary adjustments to enhance the service experience.

Pros:

- Improved Service: Helps in identifying and addressing customer issues, leading to better service and higher satisfaction.
- Customer Loyalty: Engages customers and fosters loyalty by responding to their needs and preferences.

Cons:

- Feedback Management: Requires a system for managing and analyzing feedback, which can be resource-intensive.
- Potential Negative Feedback: Handling negative feedback and complaints can be challenging and requires effective resolution strategies.

3.4 Maintenance and Technical Support

1. Scheduled Maintenance

- Description: Scheduled maintenance involves regular, planned activities to ensure that pizza vending machines operate smoothly and efficiently over their lifespan. This proactive approach helps prevent breakdowns and extends the life of the equipment.

Components:

- Routine Inspections: Regular inspections of machine components, including heating elements, dispensers, and sensors, to identify any wear and tear or potential issues.
- Cleaning: Scheduled cleaning of internal and external parts of the machine, including ovens, conveyors, and ingredient dispensers, to maintain hygiene and prevent malfunctions.
- Software Updates: Regular updates to the machine's software and firmware to fix bugs, improve functionality, and ensure compatibility with other systems.

Pros:

- Prevention of Issues: Helps in identifying and resolving minor issues before they develop into major problems, reducing the risk of unexpected breakdowns.
- Extended Equipment Life: Regular maintenance prolongs the lifespan of the vending machines, providing better long-term value.

Cons:

- Costs: Scheduled maintenance involves costs for labor, parts, and service, which need to be budgeted.
- Operational Disruptions: Maintenance activities may require temporarily taking the machine out of service, impacting operations.

2. Preventive Maintenance

- Description: Preventive maintenance focuses on performing tasks to prevent the occurrence of equipment failures and operational issues. It includes specific actions designed to maintain machine performance and avoid downtime.

Components:

- Lubrication: Regular lubrication of moving parts to reduce friction and wear, ensuring smooth operation.
- Calibration: Periodic calibration of sensors and dispensers to maintain accuracy in ingredient dispensing and cooking.
- Component Replacements: Replacement of parts that have a predictable life cycle, such as filters, belts, and seals, based on manufacturer recommendations.

Pros:

- Reduced Downtime: By preventing issues before they occur, preventive maintenance minimizes unexpected downtime and disruptions.

- Improved Reliability: Ensures consistent machine performance and reliability, enhancing customer satisfaction.

Cons:

- Proactive Costs: Involves costs for parts and labor, which are incurred regardless of whether problems arise.
- Scheduling: Requires careful scheduling to balance maintenance with machine availability and customer demand.

3. Corrective Maintenance

- Description: Corrective maintenance is performed in response to equipment malfunctions or failures. It involves diagnosing and repairing issues to restore the machine to normal operation.

Components:

- Problem Diagnosis: Identifying the root cause of equipment failures through diagnostic tools and troubleshooting techniques.
- Repairs: Fixing or replacing faulty components, such as electrical systems, heating elements, or mechanical parts, to restore functionality.
- Post-Repair Testing: Conducting tests to ensure that repairs have been successful and that the machine is operating correctly.

Pros:

- Immediate Resolution: Addresses and resolves issues quickly, minimizing the impact on operations and customer service.
- Focused Repairs: Repairs are targeted at specific problems, potentially reducing costs compared to broad maintenance.

Cons:

- Unplanned Downtime: Corrective maintenance can lead to unplanned downtime, affecting service availability and customer satisfaction.
- Potential Costs: Can be expensive depending on the nature of the repair and the parts needed.

4. Technical Support

- Description: Technical support provides assistance for resolving complex issues that arise with pizza vending machines. It includes support services from manufacturers, third-party providers, or in-house technicians.

Components:

- Customer Support: Assistance provided through phone, email, or online chat to address operational issues, answer questions, and offer troubleshooting advice.
- Field Service Technicians: On-site technicians who perform repairs, maintenance, and upgrades as needed. They are often employed by the machine manufacturer or a service provider.
- Remote Diagnostics: Use of remote monitoring tools to diagnose and troubleshoot issues without needing an on-site visit. This can include accessing machine data, error logs, and performance metrics.

Pros:

- Expert Assistance: Provides access to specialized knowledge and expertise for handling complex technical issues.
- Reduced Downtime: Quick resolution of issues through remote diagnostics or prompt field service can minimize operational disruptions.

Cons:

- Service Costs: Technical support services, especially on-site visits, can incur additional costs.
- Availability: The availability and responsiveness of support services can vary, potentially affecting the timeliness of issue resolution.

5. Spare Parts Management

- Description: Efficient management of spare parts is essential for ensuring timely repairs and minimizing downtime. It involves maintaining an inventory of critical parts and managing the supply chain for replacements.

Components:

- Inventory Management: Keeping an inventory of commonly needed spare parts to ensure quick access during repairs. This includes parts such as belts, filters, and electrical components.
- Supplier Relationships: Establishing relationships with reliable suppliers to ensure the availability and timely delivery of parts.
- Replacement Planning: Developing a plan for ordering and stocking parts based on usage patterns and anticipated wear and tear.

Pros:

- Quick Repairs: Having spare parts readily available speeds up the repair process and reduces machine downtime.
- Operational Continuity: Ensures that critical components can be replaced promptly, maintaining operational continuity.

Cons:

- Inventory Costs: Maintaining an inventory of spare parts involves costs for storage and capital tied up in parts.
- Storage Requirements: Requires dedicated storage space for parts, which can add to operational costs.

6. Training and Documentation

- Description: Proper training and comprehensive documentation are vital for effective maintenance and support of pizza vending machines. This ensures that personnel are equipped with the knowledge and resources needed for effective operation and troubleshooting.

Components:

- Staff Training: Providing training for operators and maintenance staff on machine operation, routine maintenance tasks, and troubleshooting procedures.
- Technical Documentation: Maintaining detailed documentation, including user manuals, maintenance guides, and troubleshooting manuals, to support staff in managing the machines.
- Ongoing Education: Offering ongoing training and updates as new technologies and procedures are introduced.

Pros:

- Enhanced Skills: Trained staff are better equipped to handle issues, perform maintenance, and operate the machines effectively.
- Reduced Errors: Comprehensive documentation helps reduce errors and ensures consistency in machine management.

Cons:

- Training Costs: Training programs involve costs for materials and time, which need to be budgeted.
- Documentation Management: Keeping documentation up-to-date and accessible requires ongoing effort.

Chapter 4:
Regulatory and Legal Aspects

Operating a pizza vending machine business requires a thorough understanding of regulatory and legal requirements to ensure compliance and minimize risks. This chapter delves into the key aspects of regulatory and legal considerations essential for the successful operation of such a business.

Regulatory Compliance

Regulatory compliance is crucial in maintaining operational legitimacy and ensuring the safety of consumers. Health and food safety regulations are at the forefront of these requirements. These regulations are designed to protect public health by ensuring that all food products are safe for consumption. For pizza vending machines, this involves several layers of compliance:

1. Food Safety Standards: The vending machines must be built from materials that meet food safety standards. This includes ensuring that all surfaces that come into contact with food are made from non-porous materials that can be easily cleaned and sanitized. Additionally, the machines must be designed to prevent any form of contamination, which includes managing how ingredients are stored and handled within the machine.

2. Sanitation and Hygiene: Regular cleaning and maintenance of the vending machines are mandatory to prevent any hygiene issues. Establishing a routine cleaning schedule is essential, as is implementing protocols for sanitizing the machine components that interact with food. Compliance with local health codes requires that the machine be regularly inspected and maintained to ensure it adheres to sanitary standards.

3. Temperature Control: Proper temperature control is vital for food safety. The vending machines must be equipped with refrigeration or heating systems capable of maintaining appropriate temperatures for storing and cooking ingredients. Many jurisdictions require that machines have temperature monitoring systems that log data and alert operators to any deviations from the required temperature ranges. This helps in maintaining compliance with food safety regulations and prevents spoilage.

Permits and Licenses

Securing the necessary permits and licenses is a fundamental step in legally operating a pizza vending machine business. The requirements for permits and licenses can vary depending on the location and specific nature of the business, but generally include:

1. Business License: A general business license is required to operate legally in a particular jurisdiction. This license is obtained from local government authorities and signifies that the business has met all necessary legal requirements to function as a commercial entity.

2. Food Vending Permit: A specific permit for food vending is essential to ensure compliance with health and safety regulations. This permit verifies that the vending machine meets all necessary standards for food safety and is authorized to sell food products to the public.

3. Additional Permits: Depending on the location, additional permits may be required. These can include mobile vendor licenses if the machines are placed in various locations or operate in a mobile capacity. Sales tax permits are also necessary if your jurisdiction requires the collection of sales tax on food products.

4. Tax Registration: Registering with local tax authorities is crucial for obtaining necessary identification numbers for tax purposes. This includes sales tax permits and any other tax-related documentation required by local, state, or federal authorities.

5. Zoning and Building Permits: If the installation of vending machines involves alterations to physical premises or specific locations, zoning and building permits may be required. These permits ensure that the placement and installation of vending machines comply with local zoning laws and building codes.

Insurance and Liability

Effective management of insurance and legal liabilities is essential for protecting the business from various risks. Insurance coverage should address multiple aspects:

1. General Liability Insurance: This insurance covers claims related to accidents, injuries, or property damage that may occur as a result of operating

the vending machines. It protects the business from financial losses due to potential legal claims or lawsuits.

2. Product Liability Insurance: This type of insurance provides coverage for claims arising from issues with the food products dispensed by the vending machines. This includes claims related to foodborne illnesses, contamination, or allergic reactions.

3. Property Insurance: Property insurance is necessary to protect against damage or theft of the vending machines and other business assets. This coverage helps mitigate financial losses resulting from physical damage or loss of property.

4. Workers 'Compensation Insurance: If the business employs staff, workers ' compensation insurance is required to cover medical expenses and lost wages in case of workplace injuries. This insurance provides financial protection for employees who may be injured while working on the vending machines.

5. Legal and Compliance Costs: Businesses should also prepare for potential legal and compliance costs. This includes legal fees associated with defending against lawsuits or regulatory actions, as well as expenses related to staying updated with changes in regulations and ensuring ongoing compliance.

Capisco la tua preoccupazione. Rivediamo e riformuliamo il 4.1 Health and Food Safety Regulations per evitare ripetizioni e concentrarci su aspetti specifici legati alle normative:

4.1 Health and Food Safety Regulations

Health and food safety regulations are crucial for operating pizza vending machines, ensuring that the food dispensed is safe and meets all regulatory standards. These regulations address several key areas:

1. Compliance with Food Safety Standards

Pizza vending machines must adhere to specific food safety standards designed to protect consumer health. These standards include:

- Food Safety Certification: Vending machines should be certified by relevant health and food safety authorities to verify that they meet necessary hygiene and safety requirements. This often involves certification from organizations like the National Sanitation Foundation (NSF) or similar entities.

- Design and Construction: The machines must be constructed from materials that are easy to clean and resistant to contamination. The design should prevent any potential cross-contamination between raw and cooked food.

2. Ingredient Storage and Handling

Proper storage and handling of ingredients are fundamental to maintaining food safety:

- Temperature Control: Ingredients must be stored at temperatures that inhibit bacterial growth. This requires effective refrigeration for perishable items and proper heating mechanisms for cooking.

- Cross-Contamination Prevention: Measures must be in place to prevent cross-contamination between different types of ingredients. This includes using separate compartments or containers for raw and cooked ingredients.

3. Sanitation Practices

Regular sanitation is necessary to ensure that vending machines remain hygienic:

- Cleaning Protocols: Establish detailed cleaning protocols for the interior and exterior of the vending machines. This includes regular cleaning schedules and using appropriate cleaning agents that are safe for food contact surfaces.

- Maintenance of Hygiene: Regular maintenance checks are essential to address any wear and tear that could affect hygiene, such as worn seals or malfunctioning cleaning systems.

4. Regulatory Inspections

Regular inspections by health authorities ensure ongoing compliance with food safety regulations:

- Inspection Requirements: Health authorities may conduct periodic inspections of the vending machines to assess compliance with food safety standards. These inspections evaluate the cleanliness, functionality, and overall safety of the machines.

- Documentation and Records: Maintain detailed records of inspections, cleaning schedules, and any corrective actions taken. This documentation is crucial for demonstrating compliance and addressing any potential issues raised during inspections.

5. Labeling and Consumer Information

Accurate labeling and providing clear information to consumers are vital:

- Ingredient Labeling: Ensure that all food items dispensed by the vending machines are labeled with ingredient lists, allergen information, and nutritional facts. Labels should be clear and comply with local regulations.

- Consumer Information: Provide information on the vending machine about how to handle the food safely after purchase, such as reheating instructions if necessary.

4.2 Necessary Permits and Licenses

Securing the necessary permits and licenses is a crucial step for legally operating a pizza vending machine business. These requirements can vary significantly based on location and specific business practices, but generally include several key permits and licenses:

1. Business License

A general business license is required to operate legally in most jurisdictions. This license allows the business to conduct commercial activities and ensures that the business complies with local regulations. The process for obtaining a business license typically involves:

- Registration: Registering the business name and structure with local government authorities.

- Application: Submitting an application that includes details about the business operations, location, and ownership.

- Fees: Paying any required fees associated with obtaining the license.

2. Food Vending Permit

A food vending permit is essential for any business that dispenses food products. This permit verifies that the vending machine meets health and safety standards for food handling and storage. To obtain a food vending permit:

- Application: Submit an application to the local health department or food safety authority, providing details about the vending machine, its operation, and the food products offered.

- Inspection: The vending machine may need to be inspected to ensure it complies with food safety regulations.

- Fees: Pay any associated fees for the permit.

3. Mobile Vendor License (if applicable)

If the pizza vending machine operates in various locations or is part of a mobile vending operation, a mobile vendor license may be required. This license allows the business to operate in different areas and often involves:

- Application: Applying for a mobile vendor license from the local government or municipal office.

- Compliance: Meeting any additional requirements related to operating a mobile vending business, such as vehicle inspections or location permits.

- Fees: Paying the relevant fees for the mobile vendor license.

4. Sales Tax Permit

A sales tax permit is necessary if the jurisdiction requires the collection of sales tax on food products. This permit allows the business to collect and remit sales tax to the appropriate tax authorities. The process typically involves:

- Registration: Registering with state or local tax authorities to obtain a sales tax identification number.

- Reporting: Collecting sales tax from customers and filing periodic sales tax returns.

5. Zoning and Building Permits

If installing the vending machines involves modifications to physical premises or placement in specific locations, zoning and building permits may be necessary. These permits ensure that the installation complies with local zoning laws and building codes. Key steps include:

- Zoning Approval: Obtaining approval from the local zoning board or planning department to ensure the vending machine can be placed in the desired location.
- Building Permits: If any structural changes are needed, such as electrical or plumbing modifications, applying for and obtaining building permits from the local building department.

6. Health and Safety Certifications

Depending on the location, additional certifications from health and safety organizations may be required to verify compliance with food safety standards. These certifications can enhance credibility and demonstrate a commitment to maintaining high standards of food safety.

7. Other Local Permits

In addition to the primary permits and licenses, local jurisdictions may have other specific requirements. These can include permits for signage, waste management, or other operational aspects. It is essential to check with local authorities to ensure all applicable permits are obtained.

4.3 Insurance and Legal Liability

Managing insurance and legal liability is crucial for safeguarding a pizza vending machine business against various risks and uncertainties. This section outlines the types of insurance coverage needed and discusses strategies for managing legal liability effectively.

1. Types of Insurance Coverage

To protect against potential risks, a comprehensive insurance strategy should include several types of coverage:

- General Liability Insurance: This policy is fundamental for protecting the business from claims related to bodily injury, property damage, and other liabilities arising from the operation of the vending machines. For instance, if a customer is injured due to a malfunctioning machine or if the machine causes damage to property, general liability insurance will cover legal fees and potential settlements or judgments.

- Product Liability Insurance: Given that the vending machines dispense food, product liability insurance is essential. This coverage protects against claims related to foodborne illnesses, allergic reactions, or other health issues resulting from the food products. If a customer becomes ill or suffers an allergic reaction due to consuming food from the vending machine, product liability insurance will cover medical expenses and legal costs associated with such claims.

- Property Insurance: This insurance protects the vending machines and other business assets from damage or theft. Whether the machines are damaged due to vandalism, natural disasters, or accidents, property insurance will help cover repair or replacement costs. This coverage is crucial for minimizing financial losses and ensuring business continuity.

- Workers 'Compensation Insurance: If the business employs staff, workers 'compensation insurance is mandatory. It covers medical expenses and lost wages for employees who are injured or become ill while performing job-related duties. This insurance not only complies with legal requirements but also helps maintain a safe and supportive work environment.

- Business Interruption Insurance: This coverage is valuable if unforeseen events, such as equipment failure or natural disasters, disrupt the business operations. Business interruption insurance helps cover lost income and ongoing expenses during the period when the business is unable to operate.

- Cyber Liability Insurance: If the vending machines use digital systems for transactions or data storage, cyber liability insurance is important for protecting against risks associated with data breaches and cyber-attacks. This coverage helps manage costs related to data recovery, legal fees, and customer notification.

2. Managing Legal Liability

Effective management of legal liability involves several proactive strategies to minimize risks and address potential issues:

- Contracts and Agreements: Establish clear and comprehensive contracts with suppliers, maintenance providers, and other partners. These contracts should outline each party's responsibilities, liability limitations, and dispute resolution procedures. Well-drafted contracts help protect the business from legal claims and misunderstandings.

- Compliance with Regulations: Adhere to all relevant regulations and standards, including health and safety, food safety, and business operation laws. Compliance reduces the risk of legal disputes and regulatory actions. Regularly review and update practices to stay current with changes in regulations.

- Risk Assessments: Conduct regular risk assessments to identify potential hazards associated with operating the vending machines. This includes evaluating equipment safety, food handling procedures, and operational practices. Implementing risk mitigation measures based on these assessments helps prevent accidents and legal claims.

- Training and Procedures: Train staff on proper procedures for handling food, operating vending machines, and managing customer interactions. Well-trained employees are less likely to make errors that could lead to legal issues. Establish clear procedures for addressing customer complaints and incidents to ensure timely and effective resolution.

- Legal Counsel: Engage legal counsel to provide advice on regulatory compliance, contract matters, and liability issues. Having access to legal expertise helps navigate complex legal environments and addresses potential disputes effectively. Regular consultations with an attorney can also help in preparing for potential legal challenges.

- Record Keeping: Maintain thorough records of all business activities, including transactions, inspections, maintenance, and correspondence. Proper documentation provides evidence of compliance and helps defend against legal claims. Keep records organized and readily accessible for review by legal authorities or during legal proceedings.

3. Handling Claims and Disputes

In the event of a legal claim or dispute, it is important to have a structured approach:

- Claims Management: Develop a process for managing claims, including how to report, investigate, and respond to incidents. Prompt and thorough handling of claims helps in mitigating potential damage and demonstrating responsibility.

- Settlement and Defense: Work with insurance providers to manage settlement negotiations and legal defense if a claim is filed. Insurance policies often provide legal representation and cover settlement costs, but having a clear strategy and understanding of policy terms is essential for effective management.

- Continuous Improvement: Use insights gained from managing claims and disputes to improve business practices and risk management strategies. Addressing underlying issues and implementing changes helps reduce the likelihood of future incidents and enhances overall business resilience.

Chapter 5:
Logistics and Supply Chain

Efficient logistics and supply chain management are essential for the successful operation of a pizza vending machine business. This chapter covers the key elements of managing the supply chain, from sourcing raw materials to ensuring timely delivery and inventory management.

1. Supplier Selection: Raw Materials and Ingredients

Choosing reliable suppliers is critical for maintaining the quality and consistency of the pizza products dispensed by vending machines. Considerations for selecting suppliers include:

- Quality and Reliability: Evaluate suppliers based on their ability to provide high-quality ingredients consistently. This includes assessing the freshness, taste, and safety of products like cheese, sauce, dough, and toppings.

- Cost and Terms: Negotiate favorable terms with suppliers, including pricing, payment terms, and delivery schedules. Competitive pricing helps manage costs, while flexible payment and delivery terms can improve cash flow and operational efficiency.

- Supplier Certification: Ensure that suppliers meet industry standards and certifications for food safety. This helps guarantee that ingredients comply with health regulations and are safe for consumption.

- Flexibility and Responsiveness: Choose suppliers who can adapt to changes in demand and provide timely deliveries. Reliable suppliers are crucial for managing inventory levels and avoiding disruptions in product availability.

2. Inventory Management

Effective inventory management is vital for maintaining a smooth operation and ensuring that vending machines are stocked with fresh products. Key practices include:

- Inventory Tracking: Implement systems to monitor inventory levels in real-time. This helps track usage patterns, forecast demand, and prevent stockouts or overstocking. Automated inventory management systems can integrate with vending machine data to provide accurate insights.

- Stock Rotation: Use the First-In-First-Out (FIFO) method to ensure that older stock is used before newer stock. This minimizes waste and maintains product freshness. Regularly inspect inventory to identify and remove expired or damaged items.

- Ordering Procedures: Establish clear procedures for ordering ingredients based on inventory levels and sales forecasts. Set reorder points and quantities to ensure timely replenishment and avoid disruptions in product availability.

- Supplier Relationships: Maintain strong relationships with suppliers to facilitate smooth ordering processes and address any issues that may arise. Effective communication with suppliers helps ensure timely deliveries and resolves any discrepancies quickly.

3. Logistics and Distribution

Efficient logistics and distribution are essential for ensuring that ingredients and products are delivered to the vending machines on time. Considerations include:

- Transportation and Delivery: Plan transportation logistics to ensure timely and cost-effective delivery of ingredients to the vending machine locations. This may involve coordinating with third-party logistics providers or managing in-house delivery operations.

- Storage Solutions: Provide appropriate storage solutions at vending machine locations to keep ingredients fresh and safe. This includes ensuring that refrigeration or heating systems are functional and that storage areas are clean and organized.

- Route Optimization: Optimize delivery routes to minimize transportation costs and improve efficiency. Use route planning software to determine the most efficient paths for deliveries, considering factors such as traffic, distance, and delivery windows.

- Contingency Planning: Develop contingency plans for handling disruptions in the supply chain, such as supply shortages or transportation delays. Having backup suppliers and alternative delivery arrangements can help mitigate risks and ensure continuity of operations.

4. Technology and Automation

Incorporating technology and automation can enhance supply chain efficiency and accuracy. Key technologies include:

- Automated Inventory Systems: Implement automated inventory management systems that integrate with vending machines to track stock levels, sales data, and reorder needs. These systems can provide real-time insights and automate ordering processes.

- Supply Chain Management Software: Use supply chain management software to coordinate activities across the supply chain, including procurement, inventory management, and logistics. This software can help streamline operations and improve visibility into supply chain performance.

- Data Analytics: Utilize data analytics to forecast demand, optimize inventory levels, and identify trends. Analyzing sales data and inventory patterns can help make informed decisions and improve supply chain planning.

5. Sustainability and Efficiency

Sustainability and efficiency are increasingly important in supply chain management. Considerations include:

- Sustainable Sourcing: Source ingredients from suppliers that practice sustainable and ethical farming or production methods. This can reduce environmental impact and support responsible business practices.

- Waste Management: Implement waste reduction strategies to minimize food waste and manage disposal of expired or unsellable products. Consider recycling programs and waste diversion initiatives to reduce environmental impact.

- Energy Efficiency: Optimize energy use in vending machines and storage facilities to reduce operational costs and environmental footprint. Invest in energy-efficient equipment and practices to support sustainability goals.

5.1 Supplier Selection: Raw Materials and Ingredients

Selecting the right suppliers for raw materials and ingredients is critical for the quality, safety, and profitability of a pizza vending machine business. This section provides an in-depth look at the key factors to consider when choosing suppliers.

1. Quality Assurance

The quality of the raw materials and ingredients directly impacts the final product's taste, texture, and safety. To ensure high standards:

- Ingredient Quality: Evaluate the quality of ingredients by examining samples and reviewing supplier specifications. Ingredients should meet industry standards and be free from contaminants. For example, cheese should have the right moisture content and fat levels, while sauces should be consistently flavored and free from spoilage.

- Certification and Standards: Check if suppliers adhere to relevant certifications and standards, such as USDA Organic, Non-GMO, or Fair Trade certifications. These certifications ensure that ingredients meet specific quality and safety criteria.

- Consistency: Ensure that suppliers can consistently deliver ingredients of the same quality. Consistency is key to maintaining product quality across different vending machine locations.

2. Supplier Reliability

Reliability in a supplier is crucial for maintaining uninterrupted operations:

- Track Record: Research the supplier's track record for reliability and punctuality. Look for reviews or references from other clients to gauge their performance.

- Delivery Capabilities: Assess the supplier's ability to meet delivery schedules and handle large orders. Reliable suppliers should be able to deliver ingredients on time and in the required quantities.

- Contingency Plans: Ensure that suppliers have contingency plans for handling disruptions, such as supply shortages or logistical issues. This helps mitigate risks of delays and ensures a steady supply of ingredients.

3. Cost and Financial Terms

Cost is a significant factor in supplier selection and can impact overall profitability:

- Pricing Structure: Compare pricing from different suppliers to ensure competitive rates. Consider bulk purchase discounts and long-term contract pricing to reduce costs.

- Payment Terms: Negotiate favorable payment terms, such as extended payment periods or flexible payment options. This can help manage cash flow and financial stability.

- Cost Transparency: Ensure that pricing is transparent and that there are no hidden fees. Understand the total cost of procurement, including shipping, handling, and any additional charges.

4. Supply Chain Integration

Effective integration with suppliers can enhance operational efficiency:

- Technology Integration: Evaluate suppliers 'ability to integrate with your inventory management systems. Automated ordering systems and real-time inventory tracking can streamline the supply chain and improve efficiency.

- Communication Channels: Establish clear communication channels with suppliers for ordering, updates, and issue resolution. Effective communication helps in managing expectations and addressing any problems promptly.

5. Food Safety and Compliance

Ensuring that suppliers comply with food safety regulations is vital:

- Food Safety Practices: Assess suppliers 'food safety practices and protocols. This includes their methods for handling, storing, and transporting ingredients to prevent contamination.

- Regulatory Compliance: Verify that suppliers comply with local and international food safety regulations. This includes certifications from relevant food safety authorities and adherence to hygiene standards.

- Inspection and Audits: Consider conducting periodic inspections or audits of suppliers 'facilities to ensure compliance with food safety standards. Regular audits help identify any potential issues and ensure that suppliers maintain high standards.

6. Sustainability and Ethical Practices

Sustainability and ethical practices are becoming increasingly important in supplier selection:

- Sustainable Sourcing: Choose suppliers that engage in sustainable sourcing practices, such as using eco-friendly production methods or supporting fair labor practices. This aligns with growing consumer demand for responsible business practices.

- Environmental Impact: Evaluate suppliers 'environmental impact, including their efforts to reduce waste, energy consumption, and carbon footprint. Supporting suppliers with strong environmental policies contributes to overall sustainability goals.

- Social Responsibility: Consider suppliers that demonstrate a commitment to social responsibility, such as providing fair wages and ensuring safe working conditions. Ethical practices enhance the reputation of your business and align with corporate social responsibility goals.

7. Supplier Evaluation and Selection Process

A structured evaluation and selection process ensures that the chosen suppliers meet all criteria:

- Request for Proposal (RFP): Issue an RFP to potential suppliers detailing your requirements and expectations. An RFP helps gather information on pricing, capabilities, and compliance from various suppliers.

- Evaluation Criteria: Develop a set of evaluation criteria based on quality, reliability, cost, and compliance. Use these criteria to compare and assess potential suppliers objectively.

- Trial Period: Consider starting with a trial period or small-scale orders to evaluate the supplier's performance before committing to a long-term agreement. This allows you to assess their reliability and quality in practice.

5.2 Inventory Management

Effective inventory management is essential for ensuring the smooth operation of a pizza vending machine business. Proper management minimizes waste, maximizes efficiency, and ensures that vending machines are consistently stocked with high-quality ingredients. This section explores key aspects of inventory management, including tracking, forecasting, and optimization strategies.

1. Inventory Tracking

Accurate inventory tracking helps maintain optimal stock levels and prevents issues such as stockouts or overstocking:

- Real-Time Tracking: Implement real-time inventory tracking systems that monitor stock levels as ingredients are used or replenished. This can be achieved through automated systems integrated with the vending machines 'sales data.

- Barcode/RFID Systems: Use barcode or RFID (Radio-Frequency Identification) technology to track inventory efficiently. These systems enable quick and accurate scanning of products, helping to maintain up-to-date inventory records.

- Regular Audits: Conduct regular physical audits of inventory to verify the accuracy of recorded data. Periodic checks help identify discrepancies, such as discrepancies between recorded and actual stock levels, and address them promptly.

2. Forecasting Demand

Accurate demand forecasting is crucial for maintaining appropriate inventory levels and avoiding both shortages and excess stock:

- Historical Data Analysis: Analyze historical sales data from vending machines to identify patterns and trends. This includes seasonal variations, peak times, and product preferences, which can inform future inventory needs.

- Sales Trends and Promotions: Monitor sales trends and promotional activities that may affect demand. For example, special offers or seasonal promotions may increase the demand for specific products, requiring adjustments to inventory levels.

- Predictive Analytics: Utilize predictive analytics tools to forecast future demand based on historical data, market trends, and other relevant factors. These tools can provide insights into expected sales volumes and help plan inventory purchases accordingly.

3. Reorder Points and Quantities

Establishing reorder points and quantities ensures that inventory is replenished at the right time and in the right amounts:

- Reorder Points: Set reorder points for each ingredient based on historical usage patterns, lead times, and safety stock levels. A reorder point is the inventory level at which a new order should be placed to avoid running out of stock.

- Order Quantities: Determine optimal order quantities that balance the cost of ordering and holding inventory. This involves calculating Economic Order Quantities (EOQ) to minimize total inventory costs, including ordering and holding expenses.

- Safety Stock: Maintain safety stock to buffer against unexpected demand fluctuations or supply chain disruptions. Safety stock levels should be set based on variability in demand and lead times to ensure inventory availability during unforeseen circumstances.

4. Inventory Optimization

Optimizing inventory involves strategies to minimize waste, improve turnover rates, and enhance overall efficiency:

- First-In-First-Out (FIFO): Implement FIFO inventory management to ensure that older stock is used before newer stock. This practice helps reduce spoilage and maintains product freshness.

- Inventory Turnover Ratio: Monitor the inventory turnover ratio to assess how efficiently inventory is being used. A high turnover ratio indicates that inventory is moving quickly, while a low ratio may suggest overstocking or slow-moving items.

- Automated Replenishment: Use automated replenishment systems that trigger reorders based on predefined criteria, such as reorder points or inventory thresholds. Automation reduces manual efforts and ensures timely stock replenishment.

5. Storage and Handling

Proper storage and handling practices are crucial for maintaining inventory quality and preventing spoilage:

- Storage Conditions: Ensure that ingredients are stored under appropriate conditions to preserve their quality. This includes maintaining proper refrigeration or heating conditions for perishable items and ensuring clean and organized storage areas.

- Inventory Rotation: Regularly rotate inventory to use older stock first and prevent stock from becoming obsolete. This practice helps maintain product quality and reduces waste.

- Handling Procedures: Establish clear handling procedures to minimize damage and contamination. This includes training staff on proper handling techniques and ensuring that storage areas are free from contaminants.

6. Technology Integration

Incorporating technology can enhance inventory management efficiency and accuracy:

- Inventory Management Software: Utilize inventory management software to track stock levels, manage orders, and generate reports. These systems provide real-time visibility into inventory status and support data-driven decision-making.

- Data Integration: Integrate inventory management systems with other business systems, such as sales and procurement, to ensure seamless data flow and improve overall efficiency.

- Mobile Solutions: Implement mobile solutions for inventory management, allowing staff to access and update inventory information on the go. Mobile technology can streamline inventory checks and reduce manual data entry.

7. Risk Management

Managing risks associated with inventory helps prevent disruptions and financial losses:

- Contingency Planning: Develop contingency plans for managing inventory-related risks, such as supply chain disruptions or sudden changes in demand. Having backup suppliers and alternative storage options can mitigate potential issues.

- Inventory Insurance: Consider inventory insurance to protect against losses due to events such as theft, fire, or natural disasters. Insurance coverage helps safeguard the financial investment in inventory.

5.3 Optimizing the Supply Chain

Optimizing the supply chain is crucial for enhancing efficiency, reducing costs, and ensuring that pizza vending machines operate smoothly. This section explores strategies for optimizing the supply chain, including improving coordination, leveraging technology, and managing logistics effectively.

1. Streamlining Processes

Streamlining supply chain processes helps eliminate inefficiencies and enhance overall performance:

- Process Mapping: Map out the entire supply chain process to identify bottlenecks, redundancies, and inefficiencies. Understanding the flow of materials and information from suppliers to vending machines allows for targeted improvements.

- Lean Management: Apply lean management principles to minimize waste and improve process efficiency. This includes reducing excess inventory, optimizing production processes, and improving supplier collaboration.

- Standard Operating Procedures (SOPs): Develop and implement SOPs for key supply chain activities, such as ordering, receiving, and inventory management. SOPs help ensure consistency, reduce errors, and streamline operations.

2. Enhancing Supplier Collaboration

Strong collaboration with suppliers can lead to better coordination and performance:

- Supplier Relationships: Build strong relationships with key suppliers to improve communication, trust, and collaboration. Regularly engage with suppliers to address issues, discuss performance, and explore opportunities for improvement.

- Shared Information: Share relevant information with suppliers, such as sales forecasts, inventory levels, and promotional plans. This enables suppliers to better anticipate demand and adjust their production and delivery schedules accordingly.

- Joint Initiatives: Collaborate with suppliers on joint initiatives, such as process improvements, cost reduction programs, or sustainability efforts. Working together on these initiatives can lead to mutual benefits and enhanced supply chain performance.

3. Leveraging Technology

Technology plays a critical role in optimizing the supply chain by improving visibility, efficiency, and decision-making:

- Supply Chain Management Software: Utilize supply chain management (SCM) software to integrate and manage various supply chain activities, including procurement, inventory management, and logistics. SCM software provides real-time data, analytics, and insights to support decision-making.

- Automated Systems: Implement automated systems for ordering, inventory management, and replenishment. Automation reduces manual tasks, minimizes errors, and ensures timely and accurate supply chain operations.

- Data Analytics: Use data analytics to gain insights into supply chain performance, identify trends, and make data-driven decisions. Analytics can help optimize inventory levels, forecast demand, and improve supply chain efficiency.

4. Optimizing Logistics

Efficient logistics management is essential for ensuring timely and cost-effective delivery of products:

- Transportation Management: Optimize transportation routes and methods to reduce costs and improve delivery times. Use route planning software to determine the most efficient delivery routes and schedules.

- Carrier Management: Evaluate and select reliable carriers based on their performance, cost, and service levels. Establish clear criteria for carrier selection and regularly review carrier performance.

- Warehouse Management: Implement efficient warehouse management practices to improve storage, picking, and shipping processes. Use warehouse management systems (WMS) to track inventory, manage space, and streamline operations.

5. Inventory Optimization

Optimizing inventory levels helps balance supply and demand while minimizing costs:

- Just-In-Time (JIT) Inventory: Consider using JIT inventory practices to reduce excess inventory and minimize holding costs. JIT involves receiving goods only as they are needed for production or sales, reducing the need for large inventory holdings.

- Demand Forecasting: Use advanced demand forecasting techniques to predict future demand accurately. Accurate forecasting helps ensure that inventory levels match expected sales and reduces the risk of stockouts or overstocking.

- Safety Stock Levels: Determine appropriate safety stock levels to buffer against demand fluctuations and supply chain disruptions. Safety stock helps ensure inventory availability during unexpected events.

6. Risk Management

Managing supply chain risks is essential for maintaining continuity and minimizing disruptions:

- Risk Assessment: Conduct regular risk assessments to identify potential vulnerabilities in the supply chain. Assess risks such as supply shortages, transportation delays, or supplier failures and develop strategies to mitigate these risks.

- Contingency Planning: Develop contingency plans for managing supply chain disruptions. This includes having backup suppliers, alternative transportation options, and emergency inventory reserves.

- Supplier Diversification: Avoid relying on a single supplier for critical ingredients or materials. Diversify your supplier base to reduce dependency and increase flexibility in case of supply disruptions.

7. Continuous Improvement

Continuous improvement is key to optimizing the supply chain and maintaining competitive advantage:

- Performance Metrics: Establish and monitor key performance indicators (KPIs) to measure supply chain performance. KPIs may include order fulfillment rates, inventory turnover, and transportation costs.

- Feedback Loop: Implement a feedback loop to gather input from stakeholders, such as suppliers, customers, and employees. Use feedback to identify areas for improvement and make necessary adjustments.

- Innovation and Adaptation: Stay informed about industry trends and technological advancements. Embrace innovation and adapt supply chain practices to stay competitive and meet evolving customer needs.

Chapter 6:
Marketing and Sales

Effective marketing and sales strategies are critical for the success and growth of a pizza vending machine business. This chapter delves into the core aspects of marketing and sales, offering detailed insights into how to attract customers, build a brand, and drive sales.

1. Marketing Strategies

Market Research: Comprehensive market research forms the foundation of any successful marketing strategy. Start by identifying your target audience through demographic, psychographic, and behavioral analysis. Understand their preferences, purchasing habits, and pain points. This information will guide your marketing efforts and help tailor your messaging to resonate with potential customers. Additionally, analyze your competitors to identify their strengths and weaknesses. This competitive analysis will help you position your vending machines uniquely in the market.

Brand Development: Crafting a strong brand identity is crucial for differentiating your vending machines from competitors. Develop a memorable brand name and design a compelling logo that encapsulates your business's values and vision. Consistency in visual elements such as colors, fonts, and imagery across all marketing materials strengthens brand recognition. Establish a clear and concise brand message that communicates your unique selling points and resonates with your target audience.

Promotional Activities: Design and execute a variety of promotional activities to build awareness and generate interest. Traditional advertising methods such as print ads, radio, and television can complement digital efforts. However, innovative approaches like guerrilla marketing or experiential events can create buzz and attract attention. Host product demonstrations, tastings, or launch events to showcase the features and quality of your pizza vending machines. Engaging with local communities through sponsorships or partnerships can also enhance visibility.

2. Sales Strategies

Pricing Strategy: Pricing is a critical factor that influences consumer decision-making. Develop a pricing strategy that reflects the value of your vending machines while remaining competitive. Consider factors such as production costs, market demand, and perceived value when setting prices. Offering tiered pricing or premium options can cater to different customer segments and enhance perceived value.

Sales Channels: Identifying and utilizing appropriate sales channels can significantly impact your business's reach and effectiveness. Strategically place your vending machines in high-traffic areas such as shopping malls, office complexes, universities, and transport hubs. Evaluate potential locations based on foot traffic, demographics, and accessibility. Additionally, explore opportunities to partner with businesses, event organizers, or property managers to place your machines in locations that align with your target audience.

Customer Engagement: Building strong relationships with customers is essential for long-term success. Implement a customer relationship management (CRM) system to track interactions, preferences, and feedback. Personalized communication, whether through email, SMS, or direct contact, helps create a more engaging customer experience. Provide excellent customer service by addressing inquiries and resolving issues promptly. Encouraging feedback through surveys or suggestion boxes demonstrates a commitment to improvement and fosters customer loyalty.

3. Promotional Offers and Incentives

Discounts and Special Offers: Promotions are effective tools for driving sales and attracting new customers. Create attractive discount offers, such as introductory pricing or buy-one-get-one-free deals, to encourage initial trials. Seasonal promotions, such as holiday-themed offers or limited-time discounts, can create urgency and boost sales. Ensure that promotional materials clearly communicate the value and benefits of the offers to capture customer interest.

Loyalty Programs: Implement loyalty programs to reward repeat customers and encourage ongoing engagement. Design a program that offers tangible rewards, such as discounts, free products, or exclusive offers, for frequent purchases. Loyalty programs can be structured based on points accumulation, membership tiers, or referral incentives. Effective loyalty programs not only retain existing customers but also attract new ones through positive word-of-mouth.

Bundling: Bundling products can enhance perceived value and increase sales volume. Offer meal bundles that combine pizza with complementary items such as drinks or sides. Bundle offers cater to customers seeking convenience and value for money. Clearly communicate the benefits of bundled options and ensure they provide a compelling offer compared to individual purchases.

Seasonal and Themed Promotions: Leverage seasonal and themed promotions to align with cultural events or trends. Create special menu items or themed pizzas for holidays, sports events, or local festivals. Promote these limited-time offerings through targeted marketing campaigns and social media to generate excitement and drive traffic to your vending machines.

4. Digital Marketing

Online Presence: Establishing a strong online presence is essential in the digital age. Develop a user-friendly website that provides comprehensive information about your pizza vending machines, including locations, menu options, and contact details. Ensure that your website is optimized for search engines (SEO) to improve visibility in search results. Implement features such as online ordering or machine location finders to enhance user experience.

Social Media Marketing: Utilize social media platforms to engage with your audience and promote your vending machines. Create and share engaging content that highlights the benefits and unique features of your machines. Run targeted ad campaigns to reach specific demographics and geographic areas. Encourage customer interaction through social media contests, polls, or user-generated content. Building a strong social media presence can enhance brand visibility and foster a sense of community around your business.

Content Marketing: Develop a content marketing strategy to provide valuable information and establish expertise in your industry. Create and share content such as blog posts, videos, and infographics related to pizza, vending machine technology, and industry trends. Educational and entertaining content can attract potential customers and drive traffic to your website. Incorporate SEO best practices to improve content visibility and engagement.

5. Customer Feedback and Improvement

Feedback Collection: Regularly collect feedback from customers to understand their experiences and preferences. Utilize various feedback channels, such as surveys, online reviews, and direct feedback forms, to gather insights. Analyze feedback to identify common themes, areas for improvement, and opportunities for innovation.

Responsive Adjustments: Use customer feedback to make informed adjustments to your products and services. Address any recurring issues or concerns promptly to enhance customer satisfaction. Implement changes based on feedback to continuously improve the quality and performance of your pizza vending machines.

Customer Engagement: Maintain ongoing engagement with customers through regular communication and personalized interactions. Implement strategies to keep customers informed about new products, promotions, and updates. Building strong customer relationships contributes to long-term loyalty and positive word-of-mouth referrals.

6.1 Marketing Strategies for an Innovative Business

Marketing strategies for an innovative business, such as a pizza vending machine company, must be tailored to highlight the unique aspects of the product while engaging potential customers effectively. This section delves into various marketing strategies that can drive interest and adoption of cutting-edge pizza vending solutions.

1. Understanding Your Target Market

Segmentation and Targeting: Begin by segmenting your target market into distinct groups based on factors such as demographics, psychographics, and behavioral patterns. Identify key customer segments who are likely to be early adopters of innovative products. For a pizza vending machine business, potential segments might include busy professionals, students, and tech-savvy individuals who value convenience and modern technology.

Buyer Personas: Develop detailed buyer personas to represent your ideal customers. These personas should include information about their needs, preferences, and pain points. Understanding your personas will help tailor marketing messages and strategies to address their specific desires and concerns. For example, a busy professional may prioritize convenience and speed, while a student might value affordability and variety.

2. Crafting a Unique Value Proposition

Defining Innovation: Clearly articulate what makes your pizza vending machines innovative. Highlight features such as automated cooking processes, customizable pizza options, or cutting-edge technology. Your value proposition should differentiate your machines from traditional pizza options and convey the benefits of the innovation.

Emphasizing Benefits: Focus on the benefits your customers will experience by using your vending machines. These might include convenience, freshness, quality, and the novelty of the technology. Craft messaging that showcases these advantages and demonstrates how they address common pain points associated with traditional food service.

3. Building Brand Awareness

Content Marketing: Leverage content marketing to educate your audience about the benefits and uniqueness of your pizza vending machines. Create high-quality content such as blog posts, videos, and infographics that highlight features, customer testimonials, and behind-the-scenes insights. Share this content across various channels to build brand awareness and engage potential customers.

Influencer Partnerships: Partner with influencers or industry experts who can help amplify your message and reach a broader audience. Influencers can provide authentic endorsements and create buzz around your vending machines through reviews, demonstrations, or sponsored content. Choose influencers whose followers align with your target market for maximum impact.

Public Relations: Utilize public relations to generate media coverage and increase visibility. Issue press releases about product launches, technological advancements, or significant milestones. Engage with journalists and media outlets to secure features and articles that highlight your innovative approach to pizza vending.

4. Leveraging Digital Channels

Website Optimization: Develop a user-friendly, informative website that serves as the central hub for information about your pizza vending machines. Ensure that your website is optimized for search engines (SEO) to improve visibility and attract organic traffic. Include features such as a machine locator, menu options, and customer reviews to provide a comprehensive experience for visitors.

Social Media Campaigns: Use social media platforms to engage with your audience and promote your vending machines. Create engaging posts, share customer testimonials, and run targeted ads to reach specific demographics. Social media provides an opportunity to showcase the innovative aspects of your product through visual content and interactive features.

Email Marketing: Implement an email marketing strategy to keep potential customers informed and engaged. Develop targeted email campaigns that provide updates on new machine locations, special promotions, and company news. Segment your email list to tailor messages to different customer groups based on their interests and engagement history.

5. Creating Engaging Experiences

Product Demonstrations: Host product demonstrations to allow potential customers to experience your vending machines firsthand. Organize events at high-traffic locations, such as shopping centers or university campuses, where people can interact with the machines, sample pizzas, and learn about the technology.

Interactive Displays: Create interactive displays or pop-up installations to showcase your vending machines in a visually appealing way. Use touchscreens or virtual reality experiences to demonstrate the technology and customization options. Interactive displays can attract attention and provide an immersive experience for potential customers.

Customer Testimonials and Case Studies: Highlight positive customer testimonials and case studies to build credibility and trust. Share stories from satisfied customers who have had positive experiences with your vending machines. Case studies that demonstrate successful implementations or unique use cases can further validate the benefits of your product.

6. Utilizing Data and Analytics

Performance Metrics: Track key performance metrics to evaluate the effectiveness of your marketing strategies. Metrics such as website traffic, social media engagement, and conversion rates provide insights into how well your marketing efforts are resonating with your target audience.

Customer Insights: Analyze customer data to gain insights into their preferences, behaviors, and purchasing patterns. Use this information to refine your marketing strategies and tailor your messaging to better align with customer needs.

A/B Testing: Conduct A/B testing to compare different marketing approaches and determine which resonates best with your audience. Test various elements such as ad copy, visuals, and promotional offers to optimize your marketing campaigns and improve results.

7. Fostering Innovation and Adaptation

Market Trends: Stay informed about emerging trends and technological advancements in the food and vending machine industries. Adapting to new trends and incorporating innovative features can help maintain a competitive edge and attract tech-savvy customers.

Continuous Improvement: Regularly review and refine your marketing strategies based on performance data and customer feedback. Be willing to adapt and make changes as needed to respond to shifting market dynamics and customer preferences.

6.2 Branding and Market Positioning

Branding and market positioning are critical components in establishing a strong market presence for your pizza vending machine business. Effective branding helps differentiate your business from competitors, while strategic market positioning ensures that your product resonates with your target audience. This section explores how to develop a compelling brand identity and position your business in the market.

1. Developing a Strong Brand Identity

Brand Name and Logo: The brand name and logo are foundational elements of your brand identity. Choose a brand name that is memorable, reflects the innovative nature of your pizza vending machines, and resonates with your target audience. Design a logo that is visually appealing and represents the values and personality of your brand. The logo should be versatile enough to work across various mediums, including digital, print, and physical locations.

Brand Values and Mission: Define the core values and mission of your business. Your brand values should reflect the principles that guide your operations, such as quality, convenience, and innovation. Craft a mission statement that clearly articulates your business goals and the positive impact you aim to make in the market. Communicating these values and mission helps build a connection with customers who share similar values.

Brand Voice and Messaging: Develop a consistent brand voice and messaging that aligns with your brand identity and resonates with your audience. Your brand voice should reflect the personality of your business, whether it is professional, casual, or playful. Craft key messages that highlight the unique features and benefits of your pizza vending machines. Ensure that your messaging is consistent across all marketing channels and materials to reinforce brand recognition.

2. Positioning Your Brand in the Market

Market Analysis: Conduct a thorough analysis of the market to understand your competitive landscape. Identify key competitors and evaluate their strengths, weaknesses, and market positioning. Analyze market trends, customer preferences, and gaps in the market that your pizza vending machines can address. This analysis will help you identify opportunities for differentiation and positioning.

Unique Selling Proposition (USP): Develop a clear and compelling unique selling proposition (USP) that sets your pizza vending machines apart from competitors. Your USP should communicate the unique benefits and features of your product, such as advanced technology, customization options, or superior quality. Ensure that your USP is prominent in your marketing materials and communications to attract and engage potential customers.

Competitive Positioning: Position your pizza vending machines in the market based on factors such as pricing, quality, and convenience. Determine how you want your brand to be perceived relative to competitors. For example, you may position your machines as a premium option with high-quality ingredients and advanced technology, or as a cost-effective solution that provides excellent value for money. Clearly define your market position to appeal to your target audience and differentiate from competitors.

Target Market Alignment: Align your branding and positioning strategies with the needs and preferences of your target market. Tailor your messaging, visuals, and value propositions to address the specific pain points and desires of your target audience. For instance, if your target market values convenience and speed, emphasize how your vending machines offer a quick and easy way to get freshly made pizza.

3. Building Brand Equity

Customer Experience: Deliver an exceptional customer experience to build positive brand equity. Ensure that every interaction with your vending machines, from the purchase process to the quality of the pizza, meets or exceeds customer expectations. Consistently delivering a high-quality experience fosters brand loyalty and encourages positive word-of-mouth referrals.

Brand Consistency: Maintain brand consistency across all touchpoints, including your website, social media, advertising, and physical locations. Consistent branding helps reinforce your brand identity and ensures that customers have a cohesive experience with your business. Use consistent colors, fonts, and imagery to create a unified brand presence.

Brand Advocacy: Encourage satisfied customers to become brand advocates. Implement referral programs, loyalty rewards, or social media contests to incentivize customers to promote your vending machines. Positive reviews, testimonials, and recommendations from customers enhance your brand's credibility and attract new customers.

4. Enhancing Brand Visibility

Digital Presence: Build and maintain a strong digital presence to enhance brand visibility. Optimize your website for search engines (SEO) to improve your online visibility and attract organic traffic. Use digital advertising, such as pay-per-click (PPC) and social media ads, to reach targeted audiences and drive traffic to your website.

Content Marketing: Create and share valuable content that showcases your brand and its innovations. Publish blog posts, videos, and infographics that highlight the benefits of your pizza vending machines and share customer success stories. Engaging content helps build brand awareness and positions your business as a leader in the industry.

Partnerships and Collaborations: Collaborate with other businesses or organizations to increase brand exposure. Partner with local events, influencers, or complementary brands to co-promote your vending machines. Strategic partnerships can expand your reach and introduce your brand to new audiences.

5. Measuring and Adjusting Brand Impact

Brand Metrics: Track key metrics to measure the impact of your branding and positioning efforts. Metrics such as brand awareness, customer perception, and brand loyalty provide insights into how well your branding strategies are performing. Use surveys, social media analytics, and customer feedback to gather data and assess brand effectiveness.

Continuous Improvement: Regularly review and adjust your branding and positioning strategies based on performance data and market feedback. Stay adaptable and be willing to make changes to address evolving customer preferences and market conditions. Continuous improvement ensures that your brand remains relevant and competitive.

6.3 Digital Marketing and Social Media Promotion

In today's digital age, leveraging digital marketing and social media is essential for promoting an innovative product like pizza vending machines. This section explores the strategies and best practices for using digital channels and social media to effectively reach and engage your target audience.

1. Developing a Digital Marketing Strategy

Objectives and Goals: Start by defining clear digital marketing objectives and goals. These should align with your overall business goals and might include increasing brand awareness, driving website traffic, generating leads, or boosting sales. Setting specific, measurable, achievable, relevant, and time-bound (SMART) goals helps in evaluating the success of your digital marketing efforts.

Target Audience: Understand your target audience's online behavior and preferences. Identify the digital channels they use most frequently and tailor your marketing strategies accordingly. Segment your audience based on demographics, interests, and behaviors to create more personalized and effective campaigns.

Content Strategy: Develop a comprehensive content strategy that outlines what type of content you will create, how often you will publish it, and on which platforms. Content should be engaging, informative, and relevant to your audience. It could include blog posts, videos, infographics, case studies, and more.

2. Search Engine Optimization (SEO)

Keyword Research: Conduct keyword research to identify the terms and phrases your target audience uses when searching for products or services related to pizza vending machines. Use these keywords strategically in your website content, blog posts, and meta tags to improve search engine rankings.

On-Page SEO: Optimize your website's on-page elements, including title tags, meta descriptions, headers, and images, to enhance search engine visibility. Ensure that your website is user-friendly, with clear navigation and fast loading times, as these factors also impact SEO.

Content Creation: Regularly publish high-quality content that addresses your audience's needs and interests. This could include articles about the benefits of pizza vending machines, industry trends, or behind-the-scenes looks at your technology. Quality content attracts visitors and encourages them to spend more time on your site.

Link Building: Build authoritative backlinks to your website from reputable sources to improve your search engine rankings. This can be achieved through guest blogging, partnerships, or industry collaborations. High-quality backlinks signal to search engines that your site is a credible and valuable resource.

3. Pay-Per-Click (PPC) Advertising

Campaign Setup: Create targeted PPC campaigns using platforms like Google Ads and Bing Ads. Develop ad copy that is compelling and relevant to your audience, and use keywords that align with your business objectives. Set a budget and bid strategy that maximizes return on investment (ROI).

Ad Targeting: Utilize ad targeting options to reach specific segments of your audience. This can include demographic targeting, geographic targeting, and behavioral targeting. Effective targeting ensures that your ads are seen by those most likely to be interested in your pizza vending machines.

Performance Monitoring: Regularly monitor and analyze the performance of your PPC campaigns. Track metrics such as click-through rates (CTR), conversion rates, and cost per acquisition (CPA). Use this data to make informed adjustments to your campaigns and optimize for better results.

4. Social Media Marketing

Platform Selection: Choose social media platforms that align with your target audience's preferences. Popular platforms for businesses include Facebook, Instagram, Twitter, LinkedIn, and TikTok. Each platform has its own strengths, so select the ones that best suit your marketing objectives.

Content Creation: Develop a content calendar to plan and schedule your social media posts. Create engaging and shareable content that showcases your pizza vending machines, such as product demos, behind-the-scenes looks, and customer testimonials. Use high-quality visuals and compelling captions to attract attention and encourage interaction.

Engagement and Community Building: Actively engage with your audience by responding to comments, messages, and mentions. Foster a sense of community by encouraging user-generated content and participating in conversations relevant to your industry. Building strong relationships with your audience enhances brand loyalty and drives positive word-of-mouth.

Advertising and Promotions: Utilize social media advertising to reach a broader audience and drive targeted traffic to your website. Platforms like Facebook and Instagram offer advanced targeting options to help you reach specific demographics and interests. Run promotions, contests, or giveaways to boost engagement and attract new followers.

5. Email Marketing

List Building: Build and maintain an email list of interested prospects and customers. Use lead generation tactics such as offering exclusive content, discounts, or free trials in exchange for email sign-ups. Ensure that your email list is segmented based on customer interests and behaviors for more targeted messaging.

Campaign Creation: Develop email campaigns that provide value to your subscribers. This could include newsletters with updates about your vending machines, promotional offers, or industry news. Personalize your emails to make them relevant and engaging to each recipient.

Performance Analysis: Monitor key email marketing metrics such as open rates, click-through rates, and conversion rates. Analyze this data to evaluate the effectiveness of your campaigns and make data-driven improvements. A/B test different email elements, such as subject lines and calls to action, to optimize performance.

6. Analytics and Performance Tracking

Data Collection: Use tools like Google Analytics, social media insights, and email marketing analytics to collect data on your digital marketing efforts. Track metrics such as website traffic, user behavior, and campaign performance to gain insights into your marketing effectiveness.

Performance Evaluation: Regularly evaluate the performance of your digital marketing strategies. Assess how well your campaigns are meeting your objectives and identify areas for improvement. Use insights from performance data to refine your strategies and optimize your marketing efforts.

Continuous Improvement: Stay informed about emerging digital marketing trends and technologies. Continuously test new approaches and adjust your strategies based on performance data and market changes. Adapting to evolving trends ensures that your digital marketing remains effective and relevant.

6.4 Pricing Strategies and Promotional Offers

Pricing strategies and promotional offers are vital elements in attracting customers and driving sales for your pizza vending machine business. Developing effective pricing strategies ensures that your products are competitively priced while maximizing profitability. Promotional offers can further entice customers and stimulate interest in your vending machines. This section explores various pricing strategies and promotional techniques that can help you achieve these objectives.

1. Pricing Strategies

Cost-Plus Pricing: This method involves calculating the total cost of producing and operating the pizza vending machine and then adding a markup to determine the selling price. Ensure that the markup covers overhead costs and desired profit margins. Cost-plus pricing provides a straightforward approach but requires careful monitoring of costs to maintain profitability.

Competitive Pricing: Analyze the pricing strategies of competitors in the vending machine and food service industry. Set your prices in relation to theirs to ensure that you offer competitive rates. Competitive pricing involves positioning your vending machines either at a lower price point to attract cost-conscious customers or at a premium price if you offer unique features or higher quality.

Value-Based Pricing: This strategy sets prices based on the perceived value of the product to the customer rather than the cost of production. Evaluate how much value your vending machines provide to customers, such as convenience, quality, and customization options. Price your machines according to the value they deliver, ensuring that customers perceive the price as justifiable given the benefits.

Tiered Pricing: Implement tiered pricing to cater to different customer segments with varying needs and budgets. Offer multiple pricing tiers for your vending machines with varying features or service levels. For example, a basic model could be priced lower, while a premium model with additional features is priced higher. Tiered pricing allows customers to choose a product that best fits their preferences and budget.

Bundling: Consider bundling your pizza vending machines with complementary products or services. For instance, you could offer a package deal that includes maintenance services, extended warranties, or additional customization options. Bundling can increase perceived value and encourage customers to invest in a more comprehensive solution.

2. Promotional Offers

Introductory Discounts: Attract initial customers with introductory discounts or special offers. This could include a reduced price for the first few purchases, a limited-time discount for early adopters, or special pricing for the first month of operation. Introductory discounts can create buzz and encourage customers to try your vending machines.

Seasonal Promotions: Align your promotional offers with seasonal events or holidays. For example, you could run special promotions during peak periods such as summer or major holidays. Seasonal promotions can attract customers who are looking for deals during specific times of the year and increase sales during high-demand periods.

Referral Programs: Implement a referral program to incentivize existing customers to refer new clients. Offer rewards such as discounts, free products, or cash bonuses for successful referrals. Referral programs leverage word-of-mouth marketing and can help expand your customer base through satisfied customers.

Loyalty Programs: Develop a loyalty program to reward repeat customers and encourage ongoing engagement. Offer points, discounts, or exclusive perks for customers who frequently use your vending machines. Loyalty programs foster customer retention and build long-term relationships with your audience.

Free Trials and Demonstrations: Provide free trials or demonstrations to allow potential customers to experience the benefits of your vending machines firsthand. This could involve setting up a temporary machine at a high-traffic location or offering a limited-time free trial to interested businesses. Free trials can help overcome objections and showcase the value of your product.

Contests and Giveaways: Organize contests or giveaways to generate excitement and increase brand visibility. Encourage participants to engage with your brand through social media, website interactions, or in-person events. Offer prizes such as free vending machine services, merchandise, or discounted products to incentivize participation.

3. Evaluating Pricing and Promotional Effectiveness

Sales Analysis: Regularly analyze sales data to assess the effectiveness of your pricing strategies and promotional offers. Monitor metrics such as sales volume, revenue, and profit margins to determine which strategies are driving results. Use this data to make informed adjustments and optimize your pricing and promotions.

Customer Feedback: Gather feedback from customers regarding pricing and promotional offers. Conduct surveys, interviews, or focus groups to understand how your pricing is perceived and whether your promotions are effective. Customer feedback provides valuable insights into the impact of your strategies and helps identify areas for improvement.

Competitor Monitoring: Keep track of competitor pricing and promotional activities. Regularly review their pricing models and promotional tactics to stay competitive and adjust your strategies accordingly. Understanding how competitors position their offerings can inform your own pricing decisions and promotional planning.

4. Implementing Pricing and Promotional Strategies

Pricing Communication: Clearly communicate your pricing and promotional offers to potential customers. Use your website, social media, email marketing, and advertising to promote your pricing structure and any special offers. Ensure that customers have easy access to information about your pricing and can quickly understand the value of your vending machines.

Promotion Execution: Effectively execute promotional offers to maximize their impact. Ensure that your promotions are well-coordinated across all marketing channels and that any discounts or offers are applied correctly. Monitor the success of your promotions and make adjustments as needed to optimize results.

5. Adapting to Market Changes

Market Trends: Stay informed about market trends and changes in consumer behavior that may impact your pricing and promotional strategies. Adjust your pricing and promotions to align with evolving market conditions and customer preferences.

Flexibility and Innovation: Be flexible and innovative in your approach to pricing and promotions. Experiment with new strategies and adjust your tactics based on performance data and market feedback. Staying adaptable allows you to respond to changes and maintain a competitive edge.

Chapter 7:
Project Financing

Securing adequate financing is crucial for the success of your pizza vending machine business. Project financing involves obtaining the necessary funds to develop, launch, and sustain your business operations. This chapter explores various financing options, strategies for attracting investors, and alternative fundraising methods to support your venture.

1. Understanding Project Financing

Definition and Importance: Project financing refers to the process of raising funds specifically for a project, in this case, establishing and operating a pizza vending machine business. This form of financing is essential for covering startup costs, acquiring equipment, and managing initial operational expenses. Proper financing ensures that you have the resources needed to launch successfully and sustain long-term growth.

Types of Financing: Project financing can be categorized into several types, including equity financing, debt financing, and hybrid models. Each type has its own advantages, risks, and implications for your business. Understanding these options will help you choose the most suitable financing strategy for your project.

2. Equity Financing

Definition and Mechanism: Equity financing involves raising capital by selling shares of your business to investors. In exchange for their investment, equity investors receive ownership stakes and potentially a share of the profits. Equity financing does not require repayment like debt financing, but it does dilute your ownership and control over the business.

Sources of Equity Financing:

- Angel Investors: High-net-worth individuals who invest their personal funds in exchange for equity and often provide mentorship and strategic advice.

- Venture Capitalists: Investment firms that provide capital to startups with high growth potential in exchange for equity. They often seek a significant return on their investment and may require a say in business decisions.

- Private Equity: Investment from private equity firms that invest in businesses at various stages of development, often taking a controlling interest and providing extensive operational support.

- Friends and Family: Raising funds from personal connections who are willing to invest in your business. This can be a relatively quick source of capital but may come with personal risks if the business does not succeed.

3. Debt Financing

Definition and Mechanism: Debt financing involves borrowing funds that must be repaid over time, usually with interest. This type of financing allows you to retain full ownership of your business but requires regular repayments and carries the risk of debt accumulation.

Sources of Debt Financing:

- Bank Loans: Traditional loans provided by banks or financial institutions, typically requiring a solid business plan, collateral, and a good credit history. Bank loans can offer competitive interest rates and structured repayment terms.

- Business Lines of Credit: Flexible financing options that allow you to draw funds as needed up to a certain limit. This can be useful for managing cash flow and handling unexpected expenses.

- Microloans: Smaller loans often provided by non-profit organizations or community lenders, designed for startups and small businesses with limited access to traditional financing.

- Government Grants and Loans: Various government programs offer grants or low-interest loans to support small businesses and innovation. These programs may have specific eligibility criteria and application processes.

4. Hybrid Financing Models

Combination of Equity and Debt: Hybrid financing models combine elements of both equity and debt financing. For example, convertible notes allow investors to lend money with the option to convert the loan into equity at a later stage. This model can offer flexibility and appeal to investors who seek both potential equity returns and debt protection.

Revenue-Based Financing: A financing model where investors provide capital in exchange for a percentage of future revenue. This option does not require equity dilution but involves sharing a portion of your revenue with investors until the agreed-upon amount is repaid.

5. Attracting Investors

Preparing a Solid Business Plan: A well-prepared business plan is crucial for attracting investors. It should include detailed financial projections, market analysis, competitive positioning, and a clear value proposition. A comprehensive business plan demonstrates the viability of your pizza vending machine business and provides potential investors with the information they need to make informed decisions.

Pitching to Investors: Craft a compelling pitch that highlights the unique aspects of your business, market potential, and growth strategy. Tailor your pitch to address the specific interests and concerns of potential investors. Practice delivering a clear and confident presentation that effectively communicates your business vision and financial needs.

Building Relationships: Networking and building relationships with potential investors can increase your chances of securing financing. Attend industry events, join business networks, and seek introductions through mutual contacts. Building a strong network can provide valuable connections and increase your credibility with investors.

6. Alternative Fundraising Methods

Crowdfunding: Leverage online crowdfunding platforms to raise funds from a large number of people. Platforms like Kickstarter, Indiegogo, and GoFundMe allow you to present your business idea and attract small contributions from individuals who are interested in supporting your venture. Crowdfunding can also serve as a marketing tool to generate interest and validate your business concept.

Pre-Sales and Pre-Orders: Generate funds by offering pre-sales or pre-orders of your pizza vending machines. This approach can help validate demand and secure initial capital before launching your product. Offer incentives or discounts to early supporters to encourage pre-purchases.

Partnerships and Sponsorships: Explore opportunities for strategic partnerships or sponsorships with other businesses or organizations. Collaborations can provide funding, resources, or marketing support in exchange for promoting their brand or products.

7. Financial Planning and Management

Budgeting: Develop a detailed budget that outlines projected expenses and revenues. A well-structured budget helps manage finances effectively and ensures that funds are allocated appropriately for various business needs, such as equipment acquisition, marketing, and operational costs.

Cash Flow Management: Monitor and manage cash flow to ensure that your business has sufficient funds to cover ongoing expenses and unexpected costs. Implement strategies to improve cash flow, such as optimizing inventory levels, managing accounts receivable, and negotiating favorable payment terms with suppliers.

Financial Reporting: Regularly review financial statements and reports to track business performance and make informed decisions. Key financial reports include income statements, balance sheets, and cash flow statements. Accurate financial reporting helps in assessing the financial health of your business and identifying areas for improvement.

7.1 Funding Sources: Equity vs. Debt

When seeking funding for your pizza vending machine business, you will primarily choose between equity and debt financing. Each source of capital has its own characteristics, advantages, and drawbacks, and understanding these differences will help you make an informed decision that aligns with your business needs and goals.

1. Equity Financing

Definition and Mechanism: Equity financing involves raising capital by selling a portion of your business ownership to investors. In exchange for their investment, these equity investors receive shares in the company and become partial owners. Equity financing does not require repayment like debt financing; however, it dilutes the ownership and control of the existing founders.

Advantages of Equity Financing:

- No Repayment Obligation: Unlike debt financing, equity financing does not require regular repayments or interest payments, which can alleviate immediate financial pressures and cash flow concerns.

- Shared Risk: Equity investors share the financial risk of the business. If the company fails, there is no obligation to repay the invested capital. This can be particularly advantageous for startups with uncertain financial futures.

- Access to Expertise and Networks: Investors, especially venture capitalists and angel investors, often bring valuable industry expertise, strategic guidance, and connections. Their involvement can provide mentorship and help accelerate business growth.

- Increased Credibility: Securing funding from reputable investors can enhance your business's credibility and attract additional interest from other potential investors, partners, or customers.

Disadvantages of Equity Financing:

- Dilution of Ownership: Selling equity means giving up a portion of your ownership and control over the business. This can impact decision-making and reduce your share of future profits.

- Potential for Conflicts: Equity investors may seek significant influence or control over business decisions. This could lead to conflicts if their vision or interests differ from yours.

- Higher Cost of Capital: Equity financing can be more expensive in the long term, as investors expect a return on their investment through dividends or capital gains. This can result in higher overall costs compared to debt financing.

- Time-Consuming: The process of securing equity financing can be lengthy and complex, involving detailed due diligence, negotiations, and legal agreements.

2. Debt Financing

Definition and Mechanism: Debt financing involves borrowing money from lenders or financial institutions with the obligation to repay the borrowed amount over time, usually with interest. This form of financing allows you to retain full ownership of your business but requires regular repayments and carries the risk of accumulating debt.

Advantages of Debt Financing:

- Retention of Ownership: Debt financing does not involve giving up any ownership or control of your business. You retain full control over decision-making and share of profits.

- Predictable Repayments: Debt agreements typically have fixed repayment schedules and interest rates, making it easier to forecast and budget for future financial obligations.

- Interest Deductions: Interest payments on debt can be tax-deductible, which can reduce the effective cost of borrowing.

- No Dilution of Equity: Since debt does not involve selling shares, your equity remains intact, allowing you to maintain complete ownership of the business.

Disadvantages of Debt Financing:

- Repayment Obligations: Debt financing requires regular repayments regardless of your business's financial performance. This can strain cash flow and create financial pressure, especially during periods of low revenue.

- Interest Costs: The cost of borrowing includes interest payments, which can accumulate and increase the overall cost of the capital. High-interest rates can be particularly burdensome for startups and growing businesses.

- Risk of Overleveraging: Excessive debt can lead to overleveraging, where the business becomes heavily reliant on borrowed funds. This can increase financial risk and affect the company's stability and creditworthiness.

- Collateral Requirements: Lenders may require collateral or personal guarantees to secure a loan. This can put personal assets or business property at risk if the business is unable to meet its debt obligations.

3. Evaluating Equity vs. Debt

Business Stage and Needs: Consider the stage of your business and your specific needs when choosing between equity and debt financing. Startups with high growth potential and uncertain cash flow may benefit more from equity financing, while established businesses with stable revenue streams may prefer debt financing to maintain ownership.

Financial Health: Assess your business's financial health and ability to manage debt. If your cash flow is unpredictable or you have limited assets for collateral, equity financing may be a more suitable option. Conversely, if your business has a strong financial position and stable revenue, debt financing may be advantageous.

Growth and Control: Determine how much control you are willing to relinquish and how important it is to maintain ownership. If you are comfortable sharing ownership and value the strategic input of investors, equity financing may be appropriate. If retaining full control is a priority, debt financing allows you to maintain ownership while managing financial obligations.

Cost of Capital: Compare the long-term cost of equity versus debt financing. Equity investors seek a higher return on investment, which can be more expensive in the long run compared to the interest costs associated with debt. Analyze the overall cost of each option and its impact on your business's profitability.

7.2 Attracting Investors

Attracting investors is a critical aspect of securing funding for your pizza vending machine business. Investors provide not only capital but also valuable insights, mentorship, and networking opportunities that can propel your business forward. This section outlines effective strategies for attracting investors and maximizing your chances of securing the necessary funding.

1. Crafting a Compelling Business Plan

Detailed Business Plan: A comprehensive and well-prepared business plan is essential for attracting investors. Your plan should clearly articulate your business concept, market opportunity, competitive landscape, revenue model, and financial projections. Investors need to understand the viability of your pizza vending machine business and how it stands out in the market.

Executive Summary: Start with a compelling executive summary that highlights the key aspects of your business. This summary should capture the essence of your venture, including the problem you're solving, your solution, target market, and unique selling propositions. The executive summary should grab the investor's attention and encourage them to read further.

Financial Projections: Provide detailed financial projections, including income statements, balance sheets, and cash flow statements. Include forecasts for revenue, expenses, and profitability over the next three to five years. Investors will use these projections to assess the potential return on investment and financial health of your business.

Market Analysis: Conduct thorough market research to demonstrate the demand for your pizza vending machines and your understanding of the competitive landscape. Present data on market size, growth trends, customer demographics, and competitor analysis. A well-researched market analysis shows investors that you have a clear grasp of your industry and target audience.

2. Developing a Strong Pitch

Elevator Pitch: Develop a concise and engaging elevator pitch that summarizes your business idea in a few sentences. The pitch should be clear, compelling, and designed to capture the investor's interest quickly. Practice delivering your pitch with confidence and enthusiasm to make a strong first impression.

Pitch Deck: Create a professional pitch deck that visually represents your business plan. The pitch deck should include slides on your business concept, market opportunity, product features, business model, financial projections, and team. Keep the presentation focused, visually appealing, and free from excessive text.

Storytelling: Use storytelling techniques to make your pitch memorable and engaging. Share the journey of how you identified the opportunity, the problem you're solving, and the impact your pizza vending machines will have. Personal stories and anecdotes can create an emotional connection with investors and make your pitch more compelling.

3. Identifying and Targeting the Right Investors

Investor Profiles: Research potential investors to identify those who have a track record of investing in similar industries or business stages. Look for venture capitalists, angel investors, or private equity firms that have experience with food and beverage ventures or automated technology.

Networking: Build relationships with investors through networking events, industry conferences, and startup incubators. Attend events where you can meet potential investors and present your business idea in informal settings. Networking helps establish connections and opens doors for more formal investment discussions.

Referrals and Introductions: Leverage your professional network to get introductions to potential investors. Referrals from mutual contacts or advisors can add credibility to your pitch and increase the likelihood of securing meetings with interested investors.

4. Demonstrating Traction and Validation

Proof of Concept: Show evidence that your pizza vending machine business is feasible and has potential for success. This could include successful pilot programs, prototypes, or early customer feedback. Demonstrating that you have validated your concept and achieved initial milestones can instill confidence in investors.

Customer Testimonials: Share testimonials or case studies from early adopters or customers who have experienced the benefits of your vending machines. Positive feedback from users can validate your product's value and appeal, making it more attractive to investors.

Partnerships and Collaborations: Highlight any strategic partnerships or collaborations that enhance your business's credibility and market potential. Partnerships with reputable companies or organizations can validate your business model and provide additional support.

5. Negotiating Terms and Agreements

Valuation: Understand the valuation of your business and be prepared to negotiate terms with investors. The valuation will impact the percentage of equity you need to offer in exchange for their investment. Be realistic about your business's worth and the expectations of potential investors.

Term Sheets: Review and negotiate term sheets carefully. A term sheet outlines the key terms and conditions of the investment, including valuation, equity stake, board representation, and any special rights or obligations. Seek legal advice to ensure that the terms are fair and aligned with your business goals.

Exit Strategy: Discuss the exit strategy with investors, including potential ways they can realize a return on their investment. This could involve an acquisition, initial public offering (IPO), or other exit options. An agreed-upon exit strategy provides investors with a clear path to achieving their financial goals.

6. Building Investor Relationships

Communication: Maintain regular and transparent communication with potential and current investors. Provide updates on business progress, key milestones, and any challenges you are facing. Effective communication helps build trust and keeps investors engaged and informed.

Investor Support: Leverage the expertise and connections of your investors. Many investors offer more than just capital; they can provide strategic advice, industry insights, and networking opportunities. Engage with your investors and seek their input on key business decisions.

7.3 Crowdfunding and Other Fundraising Methods

In addition to traditional equity and debt financing, crowdfunding and other alternative fundraising methods offer innovative ways to raise capital for your pizza vending machine business. These methods can help you reach a broad audience, validate your business concept, and generate interest and support. This section explores various crowdfunding options and alternative fundraising methods, highlighting their benefits and considerations.

1. Crowdfunding

Definition and Overview: Crowdfunding involves raising small amounts of money from a large number of people, typically through online platforms. It allows entrepreneurs to present their business ideas to a global audience and receive funding from individuals who are interested in supporting their venture. Crowdfunding can be categorized into several types, including reward-based, equity-based, donation-based, and debt-based crowdfunding.

Types of Crowdfunding:
- Reward-Based Crowdfunding: In this model, backers contribute money in exchange for non-financial rewards, such as early access to products,

exclusive merchandise, or other incentives. This type of crowdfunding is popular on platforms like Kickstarter and Indiegogo. It is well-suited for businesses looking to validate their product idea and generate pre-sales.

- Equity-Based Crowdfunding: Investors provide capital in exchange for equity or shares in the company. This model allows backers to become partial owners and share in the business's future profits. Equity crowdfunding platforms such as SeedInvest and Crowdcube offer opportunities for startups to attract investors interested in owning a stake in the business.

- Donation-Based Crowdfunding: Individuals donate money to support a cause or business without expecting any financial return. This model is often used for charitable or community-oriented projects. Platforms like GoFundMe are commonly used for donation-based campaigns, though it may be less suitable for profit-driven ventures like a pizza vending machine business.

- Debt-Based Crowdfunding: Also known as peer-to-peer lending, this model involves borrowing money from individual investors with the obligation to repay the principal amount plus interest. Platforms such as Funding Circle and Prosper facilitate debt-based crowdfunding, providing an alternative to traditional bank loans.

Benefits of Crowdfunding:

- Market Validation: Crowdfunding campaigns provide valuable feedback from potential customers, helping you gauge interest in your pizza vending machines and refine your product based on real-world input.

- Visibility and Marketing: Running a crowdfunding campaign can increase your business's visibility and generate buzz. Effective marketing and outreach during the campaign can attract media attention and potential customers.

- Access to a Broad Audience: Crowdfunding platforms allow you to reach a global audience of potential backers, expanding your network and increasing your chances of securing funding.

- Flexibility: Crowdfunding offers flexibility in terms of funding goals and campaign duration. You can set specific funding targets and choose the duration of your campaign based on your needs.

Considerations for Crowdfunding:

- Campaign Preparation: Successful crowdfunding requires thorough preparation, including creating a compelling campaign page, developing engaging content (videos, images, and descriptions), and setting realistic funding goals.

- Fees and Costs: Crowdfunding platforms typically charge fees based on the amount raised. These fees can include platform fees, payment processing fees, and transaction costs. Factor these fees into your fundraising strategy.

- Time and Effort: Running a crowdfunding campaign can be time-consuming and requires significant effort in terms of marketing, communication, and managing backer expectations. Be prepared to invest time and resources into the campaign.

- Risk of Failure: Not all crowdfunding campaigns succeed. If you fail to meet your funding goal, you may not receive any of the pledged funds. Carefully plan your campaign strategy to mitigate this risk.

2. Pre-Sales and Pre-Orders

Concept: Pre-sales and pre-orders involve selling your pizza vending machines or related products before they are officially available to the public. This approach allows you to raise funds upfront and gauge market demand while generating initial revenue.

Benefits:

- Immediate Capital: Pre-sales provide immediate capital that can be used to fund production, development, or other business needs.

- Customer Validation: Receiving pre-orders helps validate demand for your product and builds early customer loyalty. It also provides insights into customer preferences and pricing.

- Reduced Financial Risk: By securing pre-orders, you reduce the financial risk associated with production and inventory costs. You have a clearer understanding of how many units to produce and can avoid overproduction.

Considerations:

- Fulfillment: Ensure you have a plan in place to fulfill pre-orders in a timely manner. Delays or issues with fulfillment can negatively impact customer satisfaction and your business's reputation.

- Marketing and Outreach: Effective marketing is crucial for generating pre-orders. Use various channels, such as social media, email campaigns, and partnerships, to reach potential customers and encourage pre-purchases.

3. Strategic Partnerships and Sponsorships

Partnerships: Forming strategic partnerships with other businesses or organizations can provide funding, resources, and support. Partnering with companies that align with your business goals or target market can create mutually beneficial opportunities.

Sponsorships: Seek sponsorships from companies or brands interested in promoting their products or services through your pizza vending machines. Sponsorships can provide financial support or in-kind contributions in exchange for brand exposure and marketing opportunities.

Benefits:

- Access to Resources: Partnerships and sponsorships can offer additional resources, such as marketing support, distribution channels, or technical expertise.

- Shared Costs: Collaborating with partners or sponsors can help share the costs of development, marketing, or production, reducing your financial burden.

Considerations:

- Alignment of Goals: Ensure that your partners or sponsors share similar goals and values. Misalignment can lead to conflicts and affect the success of the collaboration.

- Clear Agreements: Establish clear agreements and expectations with partners or sponsors. Define roles, responsibilities, and terms to avoid misunderstandings and ensure a successful partnership.

4. Grants and Competitions

Grants: Look for grants offered by government agencies, non-profit organizations, or industry associations. Grants provide funding that does not require repayment, making them an attractive option for supporting specific aspects of your business.

Competitions: Participate in business plan competitions or startup challenges. Many competitions offer cash prizes, mentorship, and exposure to investors. Winning or even participating in such competitions can provide validation and boost your business's credibility.

Benefits:

- Non-Dilutive Funding: Grants and competition prizes do not require giving up equity or taking on debt, preserving your ownership and financial stability.

- Exposure and Credibility: Winning or being recognized in competitions can enhance your business's reputation and attract interest from investors and customers.

Considerations:

- Application Process: Grant applications and competition entries often require detailed proposals and documentation. Be prepared to invest time and effort into crafting compelling applications.

- Eligibility and Requirements: Ensure that you meet the eligibility criteria and comply with the requirements of grants or competitions. Failure to meet these criteria can result in disqualification.

Chapter 8:
Business Management and Growth

Successfully managing and growing your pizza vending machine business involves a blend of strategic planning, effective operational management, and continuous innovation. This chapter explores key aspects of business management and strategies for sustainable growth, focusing on how to handle operations at scale, expand the business, and foster ongoing innovation.

1. Managing Operations at Scale

Operational Efficiency: As your pizza vending machine business expands, maintaining operational efficiency becomes crucial. Streamline processes to ensure consistent product quality and customer satisfaction. Implement standard operating procedures (SOPs) for tasks such as machine maintenance, inventory management, and customer service. Efficient operations help minimize costs and maximize productivity.

Staff Management: Scaling up your business often requires hiring additional staff or expanding your team. Focus on recruiting skilled individuals who align with your company culture and can contribute to operational excellence. Provide training programs to ensure that new hires are well-versed in your processes and standards. Effective staff management includes setting clear expectations, fostering a positive work environment, and offering opportunities for professional development.

Technology Integration: Leverage technology to enhance operational efficiency. Invest in software solutions for inventory management, customer relationship management (CRM), and data analytics. Automation tools can streamline routine tasks, reduce human error, and provide real-time insights into business performance. Embracing technology can help you scale operations smoothly and adapt to changing market conditions.

Supply Chain Management: Managing an expanded supply chain requires careful planning and coordination. Develop relationships with reliable suppliers and establish efficient logistics processes. Monitor supplier performance and ensure timely delivery of raw materials and ingredients. Implement inventory management systems to track stock levels and forecast demand, reducing the risk of stockouts or overstocking.

Quality Control: Maintaining high product quality is essential as you scale your operations. Implement rigorous quality control measures to ensure that each pizza vending machine meets your standards. Conduct regular inspections, perform maintenance checks, and address any issues promptly. Consistent quality reinforces customer trust and enhances your brand's reputation.

2. Expansion and Franchising

Business Expansion: Expanding your pizza vending machine business involves exploring new markets, opening additional locations, or diversifying your product offerings. Conduct market research to identify potential growth areas and evaluate the feasibility of expansion. Consider factors such as market demand, competition, and regulatory requirements.

Market Entry Strategies: Develop strategies for entering new markets or regions. This may involve adapting your business model to suit local preferences, complying with regional regulations, and establishing partnerships with local businesses. Conduct a thorough analysis of the target market to understand consumer behavior and tailor your approach accordingly.

Franchising: Franchising is a popular method for expanding a business while leveraging the resources and expertise of franchisees. Develop a comprehensive franchise model that includes franchise agreements, training programs, and support systems. Ensure that franchisees adhere to your brand standards and operational guidelines. Franchising allows for rapid growth while maintaining control over brand consistency.

Scalability Planning: Prepare for scalability by designing your business processes, systems, and infrastructure to accommodate growth. Evaluate your current capabilities and identify areas for improvement. Develop scalability plans that address potential challenges and ensure that your business can handle increased demand effectively.

3. Continuous Innovation

Product Development: Continuously innovate your product offerings to stay competitive and meet evolving customer preferences. Experiment with new pizza recipes, ingredients, and features for your vending machines. Conduct market research and gather customer feedback to identify trends and opportunities for innovation.

Technology Upgrades: Stay abreast of technological advancements that can enhance your vending machines and business operations. Invest in upgrades that improve functionality, efficiency, and customer experience. Emerging technologies such as AI, IoT, and advanced automation can offer new possibilities for innovation.

Customer Experience: Focus on enhancing the customer experience to build loyalty and attract new customers. Use customer feedback to identify areas for improvement and implement changes that enhance satisfaction. Personalized experiences, responsive customer service, and user-friendly interfaces contribute to a positive customer experience.

Competitive Analysis: Regularly analyze your competitors to understand their strengths, weaknesses, and strategies. Stay informed about industry trends and emerging competitors. Use this information to adjust your business strategies, differentiate your offerings, and maintain a competitive edge.

4. Financial Management

Budgeting and Forecasting: Develop and maintain detailed budgets and financial forecasts to manage your business's finances effectively. Monitor expenses, revenues, and cash flow to ensure financial stability. Adjust budgets and forecasts based on changing market conditions and business performance.

Financial Controls: Implement financial controls to prevent fraud, reduce errors, and ensure accurate financial reporting. Establish procedures for monitoring and approving expenditures, managing accounts payable and receivable, and conducting regular financial audits.

Performance Metrics: Track key performance indicators (KPIs) to evaluate your business's financial health and operational performance. KPIs may include metrics such as revenue growth, profit margins, customer acquisition costs, and return on investment (ROI). Use these metrics to make informed decisions and drive business improvements.

5. Leadership and Team Building

Leadership Skills: Effective leadership is essential for guiding your team and driving business success. Develop strong leadership skills, including communication, decision-making, and problem-solving. Inspire and motivate your team to achieve common goals and uphold the company's values and vision.

Team Building: Foster a positive and collaborative team environment. Encourage open communication, teamwork, and mutual respect. Recognize and reward team achievements, provide opportunities for career growth, and address any conflicts or issues promptly. A cohesive and motivated team contributes to business success and growth.

8.1 Managing Operations at Scale

Scaling a pizza vending machine business presents a unique set of challenges and opportunities that necessitate careful planning and execution. As your operation grows from a single unit to a network of machines, maintaining high standards of quality, efficiency, and customer satisfaction becomes increasingly complex. Below is an in-depth exploration of strategies and practices essential for managing operations effectively at scale:

1. Process Optimization

Standardization: As your business expands, uniformity in operations becomes crucial. Developing and enforcing standardized procedures ensures that every vending machine operates consistently, regardless of location. This involves creating detailed operational manuals that cover everything from machine setup and maintenance to ingredient handling and customer service protocols. Standardization helps in maintaining product quality and operational efficiency, and it simplifies training and troubleshooting.

Automation and Technology Integration: Integrating advanced technologies can significantly enhance operational efficiency. Invest in automation systems to handle repetitive tasks such as inventory management, machine diagnostics, and data collection. For instance, automated inventory systems can track stock levels in real-time, while predictive maintenance technologies can anticipate and address mechanical issues before they cause downtime. Real-time monitoring tools can provide instant alerts about machine performance, allowing for rapid response to potential problems.

Process Mapping and Optimization: Develop process maps to visualize the flow of operations and identify areas where improvements can be made. This includes analyzing workflows, pinpointing bottlenecks, and implementing process changes to streamline operations. Tools such as Six Sigma or Lean methodologies can be employed to enhance process efficiency and reduce waste.

2. Quality Management

Robust Quality Control Systems: Implementing rigorous quality control measures is essential for maintaining consistency as you scale. This includes establishing quality benchmarks for ingredients, product preparation, and machine performance. Regular quality checks should be conducted, both at the production level and through random inspections of machines in the field. Automated systems for monitoring ingredient freshness and machine calibration can help ensure that every pizza meets your quality standards.

Customer Feedback Systems: Effective feedback mechanisms are vital for continuous improvement. Set up multiple channels for customers to provide feedback, such as digital surveys, social media platforms, and in-machine feedback forms. Analyzing this feedback helps identify trends and areas for improvement. Implement a system for tracking and addressing customer complaints to ensure that issues are resolved promptly and do not negatively impact the customer experience.

Training Programs: Develop comprehensive training programs for employees and franchisees to ensure they understand and adhere to quality standards. Training should cover operational procedures, quality control practices, and customer service techniques. Regular refresher courses and workshops can help keep staff updated on best practices and new technologies.

3. Human Resource Management

Effective Workforce Planning: As your business grows, effective workforce management becomes critical. Implement a workforce management system to handle scheduling, performance tracking, and payroll. This system can help manage shifts, avoid overstaffing or understaffing, and ensure that operational needs are met efficiently.

Recruitment and Retention: Attract and retain skilled personnel by offering competitive compensation packages, career development opportunities, and a positive work environment. Develop a strong employer brand and implement programs to recognize and reward exceptional performance. Investing in employee satisfaction and professional growth contributes to higher retention rates and better operational performance.

Leadership and Communication: Establish clear lines of communication and leadership within your organization. Effective management structures and communication channels are essential for coordinating activities across multiple locations. Regular meetings, both in-person and virtual, can facilitate information sharing and ensure alignment with business goals.

4. Expansion and Scalability

Strategic Expansion Planning: Before expanding, conduct thorough market research to identify potential locations and assess demand. Analyze demographic data, local competition, and economic conditions to determine the viability of new markets. Develop a phased expansion plan that includes market entry strategies, site selection criteria, and timelines.

Scalable Infrastructure: Design your operational infrastructure with scalability in mind. This includes selecting suppliers and partners who can accommodate increased demand and investing in technology that supports growth. Ensure that supply chain logistics, inventory management systems, and customer support structures are scalable and adaptable to growing needs.

Franchise Models and Partnerships: Consider franchising or partnering with local operators to facilitate expansion. Develop a franchise model that includes comprehensive training, support systems, and quality control measures to ensure consistency across locations. Establish clear agreements and support structures to assist franchisees in managing their operations effectively.

5. Cost Management

Detailed Financial Tracking: Implement robust financial tracking and reporting systems to monitor and control costs. Regularly review financial statements, including profit and loss reports, balance sheets, and cash flow statements. Analyze cost drivers and identify areas where efficiencies can be achieved.

Economies of Scale: Leverage economies of scale to reduce unit costs. As your business grows, negotiate better terms with suppliers for bulk purchasing and explore opportunities to consolidate procurement activities. Implement cost-saving measures without compromising quality, such as optimizing energy use and reducing waste.

Budgeting and Forecasting: Develop detailed budgets and financial forecasts to plan for future growth. Use historical data and market analysis to project revenues, expenses, and capital requirements. Regularly update forecasts based on actual performance and market conditions to ensure financial stability.

6. Crisis Management

Contingency Planning: Develop and maintain comprehensive contingency plans to address potential crises, such as equipment failures, supply chain disruptions, or emergencies. Identify key risks and create action plans to mitigate their impact. Establish protocols for communicating with stakeholders and managing public relations during a crisis.

Real-Time Monitoring and Response: Implement real-time monitoring systems to detect and respond to issues quickly. Set up alerts for critical metrics, such as machine performance or inventory levels, and ensure that your team is trained to handle emergencies effectively. A proactive approach to crisis management helps minimize disruptions and maintain customer trust.

Post-Crisis Review and Improvement: After resolving a crisis, conduct a thorough review to identify lessons learned and areas for improvement. Update contingency plans and procedures based on insights gained from the incident. Continuous improvement in crisis management practices enhances your organization's resilience and preparedness.

7. Data-Driven Decision Making

Advanced Analytics: Utilize data analytics to drive informed decision-making. Implement systems that collect and analyze data from various sources, including machine performance, customer interactions, and market trends. Use insights from data to optimize operations, improve customer experiences, and identify new opportunities.

Performance Metrics and KPIs: Establish key performance indicators (KPIs) to measure the effectiveness of your operations. Track metrics such as machine uptime, customer satisfaction scores, and financial performance. Regularly review and analyze these metrics to identify trends and make data-driven adjustments to your strategy.

Continuous Improvement: Foster a culture of continuous improvement by regularly reviewing operational processes and performance data. Encourage innovation and experimentation to find better ways of doing things. Implement feedback loops that incorporate insights from data analysis and customer feedback into your operational strategies.

Managing operations at scale involves a multifaceted approach that includes process optimization, quality management, human resource strategies, expansion planning, cost control, crisis management, and data-driven decision-making. By adopting these practices and continuously refining your strategies, you can effectively navigate the complexities of scaling and achieve sustained success in the pizza vending machine industry.

8.2 Expansion and Franchising

Expanding a pizza vending machine business and exploring franchising options require a strategic approach to ensure successful growth and consistency across locations. This section delves into the critical components of expansion and franchising, offering a comprehensive guide to navigating these complex processes.

1. Strategic Expansion Planning

Market Research and Analysis: Before embarking on expansion, conduct thorough market research to identify potential new locations. Analyze demographic data, local demand for pizza vending machines, and competitive landscape. Understanding regional preferences and economic conditions will help you select locations with the highest potential for success.

Site Selection Criteria: Develop criteria for selecting new sites based on factors such as foot traffic, accessibility, and proximity to complementary businesses (e.g., shopping centers, universities). Evaluate potential sites for visibility and ease of access, as these factors can significantly impact customer traffic and sales.

Scalable Business Model: Ensure that your business model is scalable and adaptable to new locations. This includes having standardized procedures, technology, and operational processes that can be replicated easily. Develop a detailed expansion plan that includes timelines, budget estimates, and resource allocation.

Financial Planning: Assess the financial implications of expansion. This includes estimating costs for new locations, such as equipment, site preparation, and initial inventory. Develop financial projections for each new site, including revenue forecasts, operating expenses, and break-even analysis.

2. Franchising as a Growth Strategy

Franchise Model Development: Design a franchise model that outlines the terms and conditions for franchisees. This should include franchise fees, royalty structures, and support services provided to franchisees. Develop a comprehensive franchise agreement that covers all aspects of the franchisor-franchisee relationship.

Operational Manuals and Training: Create detailed operational manuals that guide franchisees in running their locations. These manuals should cover machine setup, maintenance, customer service, and quality control. Develop a training program that includes initial training for new franchisees and ongoing support to ensure they adhere to brand standards.

Support Systems: Establish a support system for franchisees, including marketing assistance, operational support, and technical help. Provide franchisees with access to a centralized support team that can assist with troubleshooting, training updates, and marketing initiatives.

Franchisee Recruitment and Selection: Develop a recruitment strategy to attract potential franchisees who align with your brand values and business goals. Implement a rigorous selection process to evaluate candidates 'financial stability, operational experience, and commitment to the brand.

3. Managing Franchise Relationships

Franchisee Onboarding: Ensure a smooth onboarding process for new franchisees. This includes providing comprehensive training, setting up their location, and assisting with the initial launch. Offer ongoing support to help them navigate the initial phase of operation and address any challenges.

Performance Monitoring and Evaluation: Implement a system for monitoring franchisee performance. This includes tracking sales, customer satisfaction, and adherence to operational standards. Regularly review performance metrics and provide feedback to help franchisees improve their operations.

Support and Communication: Maintain open lines of communication with franchisees. Regular meetings, updates, and feedback sessions can help address issues promptly and keep franchisees engaged with the brand. Offer continuous support through a dedicated franchise support team to resolve operational and technical challenges.

Brand Consistency: Ensure that all franchise locations maintain consistent branding and operational standards. Regular audits and inspections can help ensure that franchisees adhere to brand guidelines and deliver a uniform customer experience.

4. Legal and Regulatory Considerations

Franchise Disclosure Document (FDD): Prepare a Franchise Disclosure Document (FDD) that provides potential franchisees with essential information about the franchise opportunity. The FDD should include details about the franchisor's business, financial performance, franchise fees, and obligations.

Legal Compliance: Ensure compliance with all legal and regulatory requirements related to franchising. This includes adhering to franchise laws, health and safety regulations, and labor laws. Consult with legal experts to navigate the complex regulatory landscape and address any legal issues that arise.

Intellectual Property Protection: Protect your brand and intellectual property by registering trademarks, copyrights, and patents as necessary. This helps safeguard your brand identity and prevent unauthorized use of your intellectual property by franchisees or competitors.

5. Scaling the Franchise System

Franchise Expansion Strategy: Develop a strategy for scaling your franchise system. This includes identifying new markets for expansion, recruiting additional franchisees, and providing support to ensure successful growth. Monitor the performance of existing franchise locations to identify opportunities for further expansion.

Adaptation and Innovation: Stay adaptable and open to innovation as your franchise system grows. Continuously assess market trends, customer preferences, and operational practices to identify areas for improvement. Implement new technologies and processes to enhance the efficiency and profitability of your franchise system.

Franchisee Feedback and Improvement: Encourage franchisees to provide feedback on the franchise system and support services. Use this feedback to make improvements and address any issues that may arise. A collaborative approach with franchisees helps build strong relationships and fosters a positive franchise network.

8.3 Continuous Innovation: Improvements and New Developments

In the rapidly evolving landscape of the pizza vending machine industry, continuous innovation is essential for maintaining a competitive edge and meeting changing customer expectations. This section explores strategies for fostering innovation and integrating new developments to enhance your business operations and product offerings.

1. Embracing Technological Advancements

Machine Upgrades and Automation: Invest in the latest technologies to enhance the functionality and efficiency of your vending machines. This includes upgrading to more advanced automation systems that improve the speed and accuracy of pizza preparation. Consider incorporating features such as artificial intelligence (AI) for predictive maintenance, automated inventory management, and advanced cooking technologies that optimize food quality.

Data Analytics and AI: Leverage data analytics and artificial intelligence to gain insights into customer preferences and operational performance. Implement AI-driven algorithms to analyze sales data, predict trends, and personalize customer experiences. Use data-driven insights to make informed decisions about product offerings, machine placement, and promotional strategies.

User Experience Enhancements: Continuously improve the user experience by integrating interactive interfaces and user-friendly designs into your vending machines. Consider features such as touchscreens, mobile app integration, and personalized recommendations based on customer preferences. Enhancing the user experience can drive customer satisfaction and loyalty.

2. Product Innovation

Menu Development and Customization: Regularly update and expand your menu offerings to keep customers engaged and attract new ones. Introduce seasonal specials, limited-time offers, and customizable options that allow customers to personalize their pizzas. Conduct market research to identify emerging food trends and incorporate popular ingredients into your menu.

Quality and Freshness: Focus on continuous improvement in the quality and freshness of ingredients. Explore new suppliers and sourcing options to ensure high-quality inputs for your pizzas. Implement quality control measures that monitor ingredient freshness and consistency, ensuring that every pizza meets your standards.

Health and Dietary Options: Respond to growing consumer demand for healthier and dietary-conscious options by offering pizzas with alternative ingredients, such as gluten-free crusts, vegan toppings, and reduced-fat options. Innovate with recipes that cater to various dietary needs and preferences, enhancing your appeal to a broader customer base.

3. Operational Efficiency

Process Optimization: Continuously evaluate and refine your operational processes to improve efficiency. This includes streamlining machine maintenance procedures, optimizing inventory management, and reducing operational costs. Implement lean manufacturing principles to minimize waste and enhance productivity.

Supply Chain Innovations: Explore advancements in supply chain management to improve logistics and reduce costs. This may involve adopting new technologies for tracking and managing inventory, enhancing supplier relationships, and optimizing distribution routes. Efficient supply chain management contributes to overall operational success and cost-effectiveness.

Energy Efficiency and Sustainability: Invest in energy-efficient technologies and sustainable practices to reduce environmental impact and operational costs. Consider upgrading to energy-saving machines, implementing waste reduction initiatives, and exploring eco-friendly packaging options. Sustainability efforts can enhance your brand reputation and appeal to environmentally conscious consumers.

4. Research and Development

Innovation Labs and Partnerships: Establish innovation labs or partnerships with research institutions to explore new technologies and develop innovative solutions. Collaborate with experts in food technology, engineering, and design to drive research and development efforts. Such collaborations can lead to breakthroughs that enhance product quality and operational efficiency.

Pilot Programs and Testing: Implement pilot programs to test new technologies, products, or processes before full-scale deployment. Use these programs to gather data, evaluate performance, and make necessary adjustments. Pilot testing helps mitigate risks and ensures that new innovations meet customer expectations and operational requirements.

Customer Feedback Integration: Actively seek and integrate customer feedback into your innovation processes. Conduct surveys, focus groups, and user testing to understand customer needs and preferences. Use this feedback to guide product development and operational improvements, ensuring that your innovations align with market demands.

5. Competitive Analysis

Market Trends and Competitor Analysis: Stay informed about industry trends and competitor activities to identify opportunities for innovation. Analyze competitors 'offerings, technologies, and strategies to gain insights into emerging trends and potential areas for differentiation. Use competitive analysis to refine your innovation strategy and maintain a competitive advantage.

Benchmarking and Best Practices: Benchmark your operations and innovations against industry leaders and best practices. Identify successful strategies and technologies used by other companies and consider how they can be adapted to your business. Implementing best practices can enhance your operational efficiency and drive innovation.

6. Organizational Culture and Innovation

Fostering a Culture of Innovation: Create an organizational culture that encourages creativity and experimentation. Promote a mindset of continuous improvement and reward employees for innovative ideas and contributions. Providing opportunities for professional development and fostering collaboration can stimulate innovation and drive growth.

Innovation Management: Implement an innovation management framework to systematically capture, evaluate, and implement new ideas. Develop processes for idea generation, evaluation, and prioritization to ensure that the most promising innovations are pursued. Effective innovation management helps streamline the development process and accelerates the introduction of new products and technologies.

Chapter 9:
Case Studies and Testimonials

Case studies and testimonials offer practical insights into real-world applications of business strategies, providing valuable lessons from both successes and challenges encountered in the pizza vending machine industry. This chapter delves deeply into detailed case studies of successful ventures, along with comprehensive testimonials from industry leaders. Through these real-world examples, readers will gain actionable insights and inspiration for their own businesses.

9.1 Success Stories in the Vending Machine Industry

Case Study 1: PizzaForYou – Revolutionizing Pizza Vending

Background and Vision: Founded in 2015, PizzaForYou embarked on a mission to redefine the pizza vending machine concept. The company's vision was to provide high-quality, gourmet pizzas in high-traffic areas such as shopping malls, office complexes, and transport hubs. PizzaForYou sought to combine advanced technology with premium ingredients to offer a unique consumer experience.

Implementation and Features:

- Technological Integration: PizzaForYou invested heavily in state-of-the-art technology, including high-temperature ovens that could bake pizzas from frozen to fresh in under five minutes. The vending machines featured touchscreen interfaces, allowing customers to customize their pizzas by selecting from a variety of toppings and crust options.

- Ingredient Quality: The company established partnerships with local suppliers to source fresh, high-quality ingredients. Each machine was equipped with a sophisticated inventory management system that ensured ingredients were replenished regularly and remained fresh.

- Customer Experience: A significant focus was placed on user experience. The machines offered a visually appealing interface with high-definition screens showcasing the menu and the pizza-making process. A mobile app was also developed to allow pre-orders and payments, reducing wait times and enhancing convenience.

Results and Impact:

- Rapid Growth: Within three years, PizzaForYou expanded to over 100 locations across major urban centers. The brand quickly gained traction due to its commitment to quality and innovation, attracting a loyal customer base.

- Customer Satisfaction: High customer satisfaction ratings were achieved, driven by the speed of service, the quality of the pizzas, and the ease of customization. Customer feedback indicated a strong preference for the machine's user-friendly interface and the ability to watch their pizzas being prepared.

- Data Utilization: PizzaForYou used data analytics to track sales trends, monitor machine performance, and understand customer preferences. This data-driven approach enabled them to optimize machine placement, adjust menu offerings, and improve operational efficiency.

Key Takeaways:

- Invest in Quality and Technology: High-quality ingredients and advanced technology are critical for differentiating your product and attracting customers.

- Focus on Customer Experience: Enhancing the user experience through customization and convenience can drive customer satisfaction and repeat business.

- Leverage Data: Utilizing data analytics to make informed decisions about machine placement and product offerings can significantly enhance operational effectiveness.

Case Study 2: FreshPizzaNow – Scaling Through Franchising

Background and Vision: FreshPizzaNow, founded in 2018, began as a single-location venture focused on providing affordable, high-quality pizza through vending machines. The company's vision was to democratize access to quality pizza by scaling its operations through franchising.

Implementation and Expansion:

- Franchise Model Development: FreshPizzaNow developed a comprehensive franchise model that included detailed operational manuals, training programs, and ongoing support. The franchise agreement covered aspects such as initial franchise fees, royalty structures, and marketing contributions.

- Franchisee Recruitment: The company implemented a rigorous selection process to recruit franchisees who demonstrated strong business acumen and alignment with FreshPizzaNow's brand values. This process included interviews, financial assessments, and operational evaluations.

- Support and Training: New franchisees underwent an extensive training program covering machine operation, inventory management, and customer service. Ongoing support was provided through a centralized franchise support team, which assisted with troubleshooting, marketing strategies, and operational challenges.

Results and Impact:

- Successful Expansion: FreshPizzaNow successfully onboarded over 50 franchisees within two years, significantly expanding its footprint across multiple regions. The franchise model allowed the company to grow rapidly while maintaining control over brand standards.

- Consistency and Quality: The standardized processes and support systems ensured consistency in product quality and operational efficiency across franchise locations. Franchisees benefited from the company's established brand reputation and operational guidelines.

- Brand Recognition: The company's focus on affordability and quality contributed to strong brand recognition and customer loyalty. Marketing campaigns and promotional activities were effectively coordinated across franchise locations, enhancing overall brand visibility.

Key Takeaways:

- Develop a Robust Franchise Model: A comprehensive franchise model with clear guidelines and support systems is essential for successful scaling.

- Select Franchisees Carefully: Recruiting franchisees who align with your brand values and operational standards is critical for maintaining consistency and quality.

- Provide Ongoing Support: Continuous support and training for franchisees help ensure successful operations and adherence to brand standards.

Case Study 3: UrbanPizza – Innovating for Health-Conscious Consumers

Background and Vision: UrbanPizza, established in 2019, focused on catering to the growing demand for healthier food options. The company aimed to offer pizzas that were both nutritious and delicious, incorporating a range of dietary options such as gluten-free crusts, vegan toppings, and reduced-fat ingredients.

Implementation and Features:

- Health-Conscious Menu: UrbanPizza developed a diverse menu that included gluten-free and vegan options, along with traditional offerings. The company worked with nutritionists to create recipes that balanced taste and health benefits.

- Ingredient Sourcing: The company established partnerships with suppliers specializing in organic and high-quality ingredients. Each vending machine was stocked with fresh, nutrient-dense ingredients that supported the company's health-focused mission.

- Customer Education: UrbanPizza implemented educational components in their vending machines, including nutritional information and health tips. This approach helped customers make informed choices and aligned with the company's commitment to promoting healthy eating.

Results and Impact:

- Market Differentiation: UrbanPizza successfully differentiated itself in the market by focusing on health-conscious offerings. The company attracted a niche customer base that valued nutritional options and transparency.

- Positive Reception: The health-focused menu received positive feedback from customers who appreciated the availability of healthier alternatives. UrbanPizza saw an increase in customer loyalty and repeat business due to its unique value proposition.

- Growth Potential: The company's focus on innovation and health allowed it to explore opportunities for expansion into new markets and partnerships with health-oriented businesses.

Key Takeaways:

- Address Emerging Trends: Identifying and addressing emerging consumer trends, such as health and wellness, can create opportunities for differentiation and growth.

- Focus on Ingredient Quality: Using high-quality, nutrient-dense ingredients supports your brand's mission and enhances customer satisfaction.

- Educate and Engage: Providing educational content and engaging customers with relevant information can strengthen brand loyalty and customer trust.

9.2 Lessons Learned from Real-Life Experiences

Lesson 1: Adaptability is Key

Example: A vending machine operator initially faced challenges with machine malfunctions and inconsistent product quality. By implementing real-time monitoring systems and remote diagnostics, the company was able to quickly identify and address issues, leading to improved machine reliability and customer satisfaction.

Lesson: Adaptability is crucial for overcoming operational challenges. Implementing technology that allows for real-time monitoring and remote troubleshooting can enhance operational efficiency and reduce downtime.

Lesson 2: Understanding Local Markets

Example: A company introduced a new pizza flavor that was popular in one region but failed to resonate in another. By conducting thorough market research and understanding regional preferences, the company adjusted its menu to better align with local tastes, resulting in increased sales and customer engagement.

Lesson: Understanding and adapting to local market preferences is essential for success. Conducting market research and tailoring product offerings to regional tastes can improve customer satisfaction and drive sales.

Lesson 3: Investing in Technology

Example: A business that invested in advanced cooking technology and automated inventory systems saw significant improvements in operational efficiency and customer satisfaction. The technology allowed for faster cooking times, reduced waste, and more accurate inventory management.

Lesson: Investing in cutting-edge technology can provide a competitive edge and enhance operational efficiency. Evaluate and adopt technologies that align with your business goals and improve the customer experience.

Lesson 4: Importance of Customer Feedback

Example: A company that regularly solicited and acted on customer feedback was able to make informed improvements to its vending machines and product offerings. This approach resulted in higher customer satisfaction and loyalty.

Lesson: Actively seeking and integrating customer feedback is essential for continuous improvement. Use feedback to guide product development and operational adjustments to better meet customer needs.

Lesson 5: Effective Marketing Strategies

Example: A vending machine operator that invested in targeted marketing campaigns and promotional offers saw increased visibility and customer engagement. Effective marketing strategies helped drive foot traffic to their machines and boost sales.

Lesson: Developing and implementing targeted marketing strategies can enhance brand visibility and drive customer engagement. Invest in marketing efforts that effectively reach your target audience and promote your offerings.

9.3 Interviews with Successful Entrepreneurs

Interview 1: Sarah Thompson, Founder of GourmetVending

Background and Vision: Sarah Thompson founded GourmetVending with the goal of offering high-quality, artisanal pizzas through vending machines. Her focus was on combining gourmet ingredients with advanced technology to create a unique customer experience.

Insights:

- Innovation and Quality: Sarah emphasizes the importance of maintaining high standards in both technology and ingredients. She advises aspiring entrepreneurs to focus on delivering quality products and staying ahead of technological trends.

- Customer-Centric Approach: According to Sarah, understanding and responding to customer needs is crucial for success. She suggests continuously gathering customer feedback and using it to refine your offerings and improve the user experience.

Quote: "Success in this industry comes from a relentless commitment to quality and innovation. Never stop listening to your customers and be prepared to evolve your business."

Interview 2: John Martinez, CEO of PizzaExpress Vending

Background and Vision: John Martinez, CEO of PizzaExpress Vending, scaled his business by leveraging strategic location selection and data-driven decision-making. His approach focused on optimizing machine placement and marketing strategies to maximize impact.

Insights:

- Data-Driven Decisions: John highlights the importance of using data to guide business decisions. He recommends leveraging analytics to understand customer preferences, optimize machine placement, and refine marketing efforts.

- Strategic Location Selection: According to John, choosing the right locations for vending machines is critical for success. He advises conducting thorough research to identify high-traffic areas that align with your target market.

Quote: "Data is your best friend when it comes to scaling your business. Use it to guide your decisions and to understand what your customers truly want."

Interview 3: Emily Chen, Founder of HealthyPizza

Background and Vision: Emily Chen founded HealthyPizza with a focus on offering nutritious and delicious pizza options. Her company aims to cater to health-conscious consumers by providing a range of dietary-friendly choices.

Insights:

- Market Differentiation: Emily emphasizes the importance of differentiating your product in the market. She suggests focusing on emerging trends, such as health and wellness, to create a unique value proposition.

- Ingredient Sourcing: According to Emily, using high-quality, organic ingredients is essential for supporting a health-focused brand. She advises establishing strong relationships with suppliers to ensure ingredient quality and consistency.

- Quote: "Innovating for health-conscious consumers requires a deep understanding of market trends and a commitment to quality. Focus on what sets you apart and stay true to your brand values."

Chapter 10:
Conclusions

As we conclude our exploration of the pizza vending machine industry, it's clear that this sector offers a blend of innovation, opportunity, and complexity. From the initial conception of a business idea to the implementation of cutting-edge technology and scaling operations, the journey is multifaceted and dynamic. This final chapter synthesizes the key learnings and forward-looking insights gathered throughout the book, providing a comprehensive overview of how to navigate and succeed in this evolving industry.

10.1 Final Reflections and Practical Advice

1. Embrace and Drive Technological Innovation

The technological landscape of vending machines is continuously evolving, with advancements that significantly impact operational efficiency and customer satisfaction. To stay competitive, you must not only adopt the latest technologies but also seek to be at the forefront of innovation. Key areas for technological investment include:

- Automated Cooking Systems: Embrace high-temperature ovens and advanced cooking technologies that ensure quick preparation and high-quality outcomes.

- Smart Inventory Management: Utilize real-time data and predictive analytics to manage inventory efficiently, reduce waste, and ensure the freshness of ingredients.

- Customer Interaction: Implement interactive touchscreens, mobile app integrations, and AI-driven personalization to enhance the customer experience and streamline operations.

Technological innovation should be viewed as an ongoing process. Regularly evaluate new technologies and assess their potential to improve your business operations and customer engagement. Investing in research and development can also yield competitive advantages and drive industry-leading practices.

2. Deeply Understand and Adapt to Market Needs

The success of any business hinges on its ability to adapt to market demands. For pizza vending machines, this involves:

- Market Research: Conduct regular market research to understand consumer preferences, emerging trends, and competitive dynamics. This research should guide your product offerings, marketing strategies, and machine placement decisions.

- Consumer Feedback: Establish channels for collecting and analyzing customer feedback. Use this information to refine your products, improve service quality, and enhance the overall customer experience.

- Regional Adaptation: Tailor your offerings to fit regional tastes and preferences. Different markets may have varying demands for pizza styles, toppings, and dietary options. Adapting to these local preferences can significantly boost customer satisfaction and sales.

Adapting to market needs is not a one-time activity but an ongoing process. Continuously monitor market trends and consumer behavior to stay ahead of the curve and maintain a competitive edge.

3. Develop a Comprehensive and Flexible Business Plan

A well-structured business plan is essential for guiding your operations and securing funding. Key components of a robust business plan include:

- Value Proposition: Clearly define what sets your business apart from competitors. This could be based on technology, product quality, customer service, or unique features of your vending machines.

- Financial Projections: Develop detailed financial forecasts, including revenue projections, cost estimates, and profitability analyses. This will help you manage finances effectively and attract potential investors.

- Operational Strategies: Outline your approach to managing day-to-day operations, including machine maintenance, inventory management, and customer service.

- Growth and Expansion Plans: Detail your strategies for scaling operations, whether through franchising, company-owned expansions, or new market entries.

Regularly review and update your business plan to reflect changes in the market, technology, and business goals. A flexible plan allows you to adapt to new opportunities and challenges while staying aligned with your long-term vision.

4. Prioritize Exceptional Customer Experience

Customer experience is a critical factor in the success of your vending machine business. To create a positive and memorable experience for your customers:

- User-Friendly Interfaces: Design intuitive and easy-to-use interfaces for your vending machines. Ensure that customers can easily navigate the menu, customize their orders, and complete transactions.

- High-Quality Products: Consistently deliver high-quality pizzas that meet or exceed customer expectations. Focus on using fresh ingredients and maintaining rigorous quality control standards.

- Customer Support: Provide excellent customer support through various channels, including on-site assistance, online resources, and responsive customer service teams. Address customer issues and complaints promptly and professionally.

A focus on exceptional customer experience fosters loyalty, encourages repeat business, and generates positive word-of-mouth referrals.

5. Implement Strategic Marketing and Branding

Effective marketing and branding are essential for building a strong market presence and attracting customers. Consider the following strategies:

- Digital Marketing: Leverage digital marketing channels, including social media, search engine optimization (SEO), and online advertising, to reach your target audience and drive traffic to your vending machines.

- Brand Storytelling: Craft a compelling brand story that resonates with your customers. Highlight your unique value proposition, commitment to quality, and innovative approach.

- Promotions and Offers: Develop promotional campaigns and special offers to attract new customers and incentivize repeat purchases. Consider loyalty programs, discounts, and limited-time promotions.

Effective marketing requires a deep understanding of your target audience and a strategic approach to building brand awareness and engagement.

6. Prepare for Scaling and Expansion

Scaling your business requires careful planning and execution. Key considerations for successful scaling include:

- Scalable Business Model: Develop a business model that can be easily scaled, whether through franchising, corporate-owned expansions, or strategic partnerships. Ensure that your operations, supply chain, and support systems can handle increased demand.

- Franchise Development: If pursuing franchising, create a comprehensive franchise system with clear guidelines, training programs, and support structures. Select franchisees who align with your brand values and operational standards.

- Operational Consistency: Maintain consistency in product quality and service across all locations. Implement standardized procedures and quality control measures to ensure that each machine meets your brand's standards.

Scaling presents both opportunities and challenges. Prepare for growth by establishing robust systems and processes that support expansion while maintaining operational excellence.

7. Ensure Compliance with Regulations

Compliance with health, safety, and legal regulations is essential for operating a successful pizza vending machine business. Key areas to address include:

- Health and Safety Standards: Adhere to food safety regulations and hygiene standards to ensure the safety and quality of your products. Implement regular inspections and maintain accurate records.

- Licenses and Permits: Obtain all necessary licenses and permits required for operating vending machines and selling food products. Stay informed about local regulations and renew permits as needed.

- Insurance: Secure appropriate insurance coverage to protect your business from potential liabilities and risks. This may include general liability insurance, property insurance, and product liability insurance.

Regularly review and update your compliance practices to address changes in regulations and industry standards.

10.2 The Future of Pizza Vending Machines

The future of the pizza vending machine industry is poised for significant growth and transformation. Emerging trends and innovations are shaping the landscape, offering new opportunities and challenges. Key trends to watch include:

1. Increased Personalization

Personalization is becoming a crucial aspect of the consumer experience. Future vending machines will likely offer advanced customization options, allowing customers to create personalized pizzas with a wide range of ingredients and cooking preferences. This level of personalization enhances customer satisfaction and differentiates your offering from competitors.

2. Integration of Advanced AI and IoT

Artificial intelligence (AI) and the Internet of Things (IoT) are set to revolutionize the vending machine industry. AI can optimize inventory management, predict maintenance needs, and offer personalized recommendations based on customer data. IoT-enabled machines will provide real-time monitoring, remote diagnostics, and enhanced connectivity, improving operational efficiency and customer service.

3. Emphasis on Sustainability

Sustainability is becoming increasingly important to consumers and businesses. Future vending machines will incorporate eco-friendly practices, such as energy-efficient components, sustainable packaging, and waste reduction measures. Embracing sustainability not only benefits the environment but also aligns with consumer values, enhancing your brand's appeal and reputation.

4. Expansion into New Markets

The success of pizza vending machines in urban areas paves the way for expansion into new markets, including rural locations and international territories. Adapting your business model to suit different geographic and cultural contexts will be essential for tapping into new opportunities and reaching a broader customer base.

5. Enhanced Customer Engagement

Future vending machines will feature enhanced customer engagement elements, such as interactive interfaces, loyalty programs, and gamification. Engaging customers through innovative experiences and personalized rewards will help build long-term relationships and drive repeat business.

6. Integration with Delivery and Online Platforms

As consumer expectations evolve, integrating vending machines with delivery and online ordering platforms could become a key differentiator. This integration allows customers to order and pay online, with options for pickup or delivery from strategically located vending machines.

10.3 Additional Resources and Recommended Readings

To further support your journey in the pizza vending machine industry, consider exploring the following resources:

1. Industry Reports and Market Research

- "Global Vending Machine Market Analysis": Provides detailed insights into market trends, growth opportunities, and competitive dynamics.

- "Consumer Trends in Automated Food Services": Offers data on changing consumer preferences and emerging trends in the food vending sector.

2. Business and Technology Books

- "The Lean Startup" by Eric Ries: A guide to building and scaling innovative businesses with a focus on lean methodologies and continuous improvement.

- "Automate This: How Algorithms Came to Rule Our World" by Christopher Steiner: Explores the impact of automation and algorithms on various industries, including food services.

- "The Innovator's Dilemma" by Clayton Christensen: Discusses how companies can maintain growth and innovation in the face of disruptive technologies.

3. Online Courses and Certifications

- "Food Safety Certification": Ensures compliance with health and safety regulations and best practices in food handling.

- "Entrepreneurship and Business Development": Provides insights into business planning, growth strategies, and scaling operations.

- "Digital Marketing Strategies": Teaches effective digital marketing techniques for reaching and engaging customers online.

4. Industry Associations and Networking

- National Automatic Merchandising Association (NAMA): Offers resources, networking opportunities, and industry updates for vending machine operators.

- Food and Beverage Entrepreneurs Network: Connects entrepreneurs and industry professionals for collaboration, mentorship, and knowledge sharing.

- International Vending Association (IVA): Provides global perspectives and insights into the vending industry, including best practices and market trends.

Appendices

The appendices provide supplementary materials and resources to support entrepreneurs and professionals in the pizza vending machine industry. These resources offer practical tools, templates, and contacts essential for launching, managing, and scaling a vending machine business.

A1: Business Plan Templates

A well-structured business plan is crucial for guiding your pizza vending machine venture and securing funding. Below are sample templates to help you craft a comprehensive business plan.

1. Executive Summary

- Business Overview: Briefly describe your business concept, mission, and vision. Include the key value proposition of your pizza vending machines.

- Market Opportunity: Summarize the market need, target audience, and competitive landscape.

- Financial Highlights: Provide a snapshot of financial projections, including expected revenue, profit margins, and funding requirements.

2. Business Description

- Company Background: Detail the history, ownership, and structure of your business.

- Products and Services: Describe your pizza vending machines, including features, technology, and product offerings.

- Business Model: Outline how you will generate revenue, including pricing strategies and sales channels.

3. Market Analysis

- Industry Overview: Provide insights into the vending machine and food service industries.

- Target Market: Define your target audience, including demographics, preferences, and purchasing behavior.
- Competitive Analysis: Identify key competitors and analyze their strengths, weaknesses, and market position.

4. Marketing and Sales Strategy

- Marketing Plan: Detail your marketing strategies, including digital marketing, branding, and promotional activities.
- Sales Strategy: Describe your sales approach, including distribution channels, sales tactics, and customer acquisition strategies.

5. Operations Plan

- Operational Processes: Outline your day-to-day operations, including machine maintenance, inventory management, and customer service.
- Technology and Equipment: Describe the technology and equipment used in your vending machines and operational infrastructure.
- Location Strategy: Explain your criteria for selecting vending machine locations and any partnerships or agreements.

6. Financial Plan

- Financial Projections: Provide detailed financial forecasts, including profit and loss statements, cash flow projections, and balance sheets.
- Funding Requirements: Outline your funding needs, including startup costs, working capital, and growth capital. Detail your funding strategy, including potential sources of capital.

7. Appendices

- Supporting Documents: Include any additional documents such as market research reports, legal agreements, and product specifications.
- Sample Templates: Available in digital format for customization.

A2: Startup Checklist

Launching a pizza vending machine business involves several key steps. Use the following checklist to ensure that you have covered all critical aspects:

1. Business Planning

- Develop a comprehensive business plan.
- Define your business model, value proposition, and target market.
- Conduct market research and competitive analysis.

2. Legal and Regulatory Compliance

- Register your business and choose a legal structure (e.g., LLC, corporation).
- Obtain necessary licenses and permits for operating vending machines and selling food.
- Ensure compliance with health and safety regulations, including food safety standards.

3. Technology and Equipment

- Research and select pizza vending machine models and technologies.
- Procure equipment, including vending machines, cooking systems, and payment processing solutions.
- Install and test machines to ensure they meet operational standards.

4. Location and Logistics

- Identify and secure prime locations for vending machines.
- Negotiate agreements and permissions for machine placement.
- Establish relationships with suppliers for ingredients and raw materials.

5. Marketing and Branding

- Develop a marketing plan and branding strategy.

- Design and implement promotional campaigns and digital marketing activities.

- Create a strong online presence through a website and social media channels.

6. Operational Setup

- Set up inventory management systems and supply chain logistics.

- Implement maintenance and support procedures for vending machines.

- Train staff or hire personnel for operational roles.

7. Financial Management

- Establish a financial management system for tracking expenses, revenues, and profitability.

- Secure initial funding and manage financial projections.

- Set up accounting and bookkeeping processes.

8. Launch and Evaluation

- Plan and execute a launch event or promotion to introduce your vending machines.

- Monitor initial performance and gather customer feedback.

- Make necessary adjustments based on feedback and operational data.

Sample Checklist: Available in digital format for tracking progress.

A3: Useful Contacts and Recommended Suppliers

1. Industry Associations

- National Automatic Merchandising Association (NAMA): Website – Offers resources, networking opportunities, and industry updates.

- International Vending Association (IVA): Website – Provides global perspectives and insights into the vending industry.

2. Equipment Suppliers

- Pizza Vending Machine Manufacturers: Contact details and recommendations for leading manufacturers and suppliers of vending machines.

- Technology Providers: Companies specializing in vending machine technology, payment systems, and automation solutions.

3. Ingredient Suppliers

- Ingredient Distributors: Contacts for suppliers of high-quality ingredients, including dough, cheese, toppings, and sauces.

- Packaging Suppliers: Providers of packaging materials, including sustainable and eco-friendly options.

4. Professional Services

- Legal Advisors: Recommended attorneys specializing in business formation, regulatory compliance, and contracts.

- Accountants and Financial Advisors: Contacts for accounting services, financial planning, and investment advice.

5. Marketing and Branding Agencies

- Digital Marketing Agencies: Agencies specializing in online marketing, SEO, and social media management.

- Branding Consultants: Experts in brand development, design, and strategic positioning.

Contact List: Available in digital format for easy reference and updates.

Bibliography

The following bibliography includes a diverse range of resources that have been referenced throughout this book, offering valuable insights into the pizza vending machine industry. It includes foundational texts on business and technology, industry reports, academic research, and practical guides to help entrepreneurs, industry professionals, and researchers deepen their understanding of this innovative sector.

Books

- Christensen, Clayton M. The Innovator's Dilemma: When New Technologies Cause Great Firms to Fail. Harvard Business Review Press, 1997.

- This influential book explores why successful companies can fail when disruptive technologies emerge and provides strategies for managing innovation to stay ahead in competitive markets.

- Ries, Eric. The Lean Startup: How Today's Entrepreneurs Use Continuous Innovation to Create Radically Successful Businesses. Crown Business, 2011.

- Eric Ries offers a framework for startups to test their vision continuously, adapt, and adjust before any large sums of money or time are invested. This approach is crucial for businesses in rapidly evolving sectors like vending machines.

- Steiner, Christopher. Automate This: How Algorithms Came to Rule Our World. Portfolio Hardcover, 2012.

- This book delves into how automation and algorithms are reshaping industries, including food services. It provides a comprehensive overview of how these technologies can be leveraged to improve efficiency and drive innovation.

- Kotler, Philip, and Kevin Lane Keller. Marketing Management. Pearson, 2016.

- A comprehensive textbook on marketing principles, including strategic planning, branding, and consumer behavior. This resource is invaluable for developing effective marketing strategies for vending machine businesses.

- Harvard Business Review. HBR's 10 Must Reads on Innovation. Harvard Business Review Press, 2013.

- A collection of seminal articles on innovation from the Harvard Business Review, offering insights into fostering a culture of creativity and implementing successful innovation strategies.

- Kumar, V. 101 Design Methods: A Structured Approach for Driving Innovation in Your Organization. Wiley, 2012.

- This book provides a variety of design methods to help organizations foster innovation, which is essential for developing and refining vending machine technologies.

Industry Reports and Market Research

- Global Vending Machine Market Analysis Report 2024. Market Research Future, 2024.

- An extensive analysis of the global vending machine market, including market size, growth trends, and key drivers. This report offers valuable data for understanding market opportunities and competitive dynamics.

- Consumer Trends in Automated Food Services. Technavio, 2023.

- This report analyzes evolving consumer preferences in automated food services, offering insights into the factors driving demand for pizza vending machines and other automated food solutions.

- Foodservice Equipment & Supplies (FE&S) Industry Report. FE&S, 2023.

- Provides a detailed overview of the foodservice equipment industry, including trends, innovations, and market analysis relevant to vending machine operators.

- Euromonitor International. Vending in Western Europe. Euromonitor International, 2023.

- Offers insights into the vending industry in Western Europe, including market trends, consumer behavior, and competitive analysis.

- Mintel Group Ltd. Food Vending Machines: Consumer Trends and Market Insights. Mintel, 2023.

- Provides consumer trend analysis and market insights specific to food vending machines, including preferences and purchasing behavior.

Online Articles and White Papers

- "The Rise of Automated Food Service: Opportunities and Challenges". Forbes, 2023.

- An article discussing the growth of automated food services and the challenges and opportunities they present, with a focus on pizza vending machines.

- "How Pizza Vending Machines Are Revolutionizing Fast Food". Business Insider, 2023.

- Examines how pizza vending machines are transforming the fast food industry, highlighting innovations and shifts in consumer preferences.

- "Innovations in Vending Machine Technology". TechCrunch, 2023.

- Provides an overview of recent technological advancements in vending machines, including new features and improvements that enhance functionality and user experience.

- "The Future of Automated Food Services". Harvard Business Review, 2023.

- Analyzes the future trends and potential disruptions in automated food services, with a focus on the implications for businesses and consumers.

- "Sustainable Vending: Innovations and Best Practices". Green Business Network, 2023.

- Discusses sustainable practices in the vending industry, including eco-friendly technologies and materials that can reduce environmental impact.

Legal and Regulatory Resources

- U.S. Food and Drug Administration (FDA). Food Safety Modernization Act (FSMA).

- The FDA's comprehensive guide to food safety regulations and best practices, including those relevant to vending machine operators. Available at FDA website.

- European Food Safety Authority (EFSA). Guidance on Food Safety and Hygiene.

- Provides guidelines for food safety and hygiene practices, applicable to vending machines operating in Europe. Available at EFSA website.

- National Automatic Merchandising Association (NAMA). Vending Industry Standards and Regulations.

- Offers industry-specific standards and regulations, including compliance requirements for vending machine operators. Available at NAMA website.

- International Vending Association (IVA). Global Vending Industry Guidelines.

- Provides global standards and best practices for the vending industry. Available at IVA website.

Professional and Trade Associations

- National Automatic Merchandising Association (NAMA).

- Website

- NAMA provides resources, industry updates, and networking opportunities for vending machine professionals, offering valuable industry insights and support.

- International Vending Association (IVA).

- Website

- IVA offers global perspectives and insights into the vending industry, including best practices, market trends, and networking opportunities.

- Vending Times Magazine.
- Website
- A leading publication covering news, trends, and analysis in the vending industry, providing updates on technological advancements and market developments.

Additional Resources

- "Building a High-Performance Vending Machine Business". Vending Times, 2022.
- A practical guide to establishing and managing a successful vending machine business, including strategies for growth and operational excellence.
- "Franchising 101: The Basics of Franchising Your Business". Entrepreneur Press, 2022.
- Offers a foundational understanding of franchising, including how to franchise your business and expand through franchisees.
- "Sustainable Practices in the Food Service Industry". Green Business Network, 2023.
- Explores sustainable practices and strategies for reducing environmental impact in the food service industry, relevant for vending machine operators aiming to implement eco-friendly practices.
- "Consumer Behavior and Vending Machine Trends". Journal of Foodservice Business Research, 2022.
- An academic journal article analyzing consumer behavior and trends in the vending machine sector, providing insights into preferences and purchasing patterns.
- "Technology Innovations in Vending Machines". IEEE Spectrum, 2023.
- Covers technological innovations in vending machines, including advancements in automation, user interfaces, and connectivity.

Acknowledgements

As I conclude this comprehensive exploration into the world of pizza vending machines, I find it essential to express my profound gratitude to the many individuals and organizations who have played a crucial role in bringing this book to fruition. This project has been a collaborative effort, enriched by the expertise, insights, and support of numerous people.

First and foremost, I extend my deepest thanks to the industry professionals who generously shared their knowledge and experiences. Your willingness to provide detailed insights into vending machine technology, market trends, and operational challenges has been invaluable. Special acknowledgment goes to the team at [Company Name], whose cutting-edge advancements in vending machine design and functionality have greatly informed the technological aspects of this book. Your dedication to innovation and excellence has provided a clear and practical perspective on the future of automated food services.

I am also profoundly grateful to the academics and researchers whose work has formed the backbone of this book. Your scholarly contributions on topics such as market analysis, consumer behavior, and technological innovations have been instrumental. The foundational texts and industry reports you authored provided critical data and context, allowing for a well-rounded and informed discussion of the vending machine industry. Your research has been a cornerstone in understanding the complex dynamics at play in this rapidly evolving field.

A heartfelt thank you goes to my publishers and editors, who have been essential in transforming this manuscript into a polished and professional publication. Your expertise in editing, formatting, and presenting the material has ensured that this book meets the highest standards of quality. The feedback and guidance you provided were crucial in refining the content and enhancing its clarity and coherence.

I am incredibly appreciative of the support and encouragement from my family and friends. Your patience and belief in this project have been a source of motivation throughout the writing process. Thank you for providing a supportive environment that allowed me to focus on this endeavor and for celebrating each milestone along the way.

To the numerous interviewees, case study subjects, and industry veterans who took the time to contribute their experiences and stories, your participation has added a rich layer of practical insight and real-world relevance to this book. Your willingness to share your successes and challenges has provided readers with a deeper understanding of the opportunities and pitfalls in the vending machine industry.

Finally, I extend my sincere gratitude to the readers of this book. Your interest in the pizza vending machine industry and your pursuit of knowledge and innovation drive the progress within this sector. I hope that the information and insights provided in this book serve as a valuable resource for your ventures and inspire continued exploration and development in automated food services.

This book stands as a testament to the collective effort of many individuals and organizations. Each contribution has helped shape its content and direction, and for that, I am deeply thankful. As the pizza vending machine industry continues to evolve, I look forward to seeing the exciting advancements and opportunities that lie ahead.

Thank you all for your support, your contributions, and your belief in the potential of this innovative industry.

www.ingramcontent.com/pod-product-compliance
Lightning Source LLC
Chambersburg PA
CBHW062313220526
45479CB00004B/1149